An Open Book

An Open Book

Angela Schuler

Published by Angela Schuler, 2022.

AN OPEN BOOK

First edition. December 22, 2022.

ISBN: 979-8215412244

Written by Angela Schuler.

I sat down to write "Thank you" cards for those who got us through this journey. They turned into this book. Consider this one big "Thank you" card.

Chapter 1

A 6 am phone call is seldom good news. Sipping on my first cup of coffee for the day, ready to scroll Facebook a while, my phone rings. It's an unrecognized number. My husband has been in the hospital now for 4 days, so I answered immediately.

"Mrs. Schuler?"

The doctor on duty at Good Samaritan hospital in Corvallis, Oregon explained to me that Scott woke up in the middle of the night with what he described as "extreme shortness of breath." He was immediately admitted to the ICU. He tells me that they are reviewing the scans that revealed a blood clot in his lung.

I begin making plans to take a shower, get dressed, and head to the hospital, a complete 180 from the plan I woke up with. You know what God says about plans though.

It's Friday. My husband's birthday is Saturday. I wasn't certain he'd be home from the hospital by then, but just in case, I was budgeting time in the day to assemble his birthday present. We have a spa that we got for free off the Facebook marketplace. It's exposed to the weather on our back deck, so I found a great deal on an adjustable patio umbrella that extends over the hot tub. It has been sitting in the box in my laundry room for weeks. Each time Scott walked by, I said, "Avert your eyes." The contents of the box were listed on the side. His birthday present, however would have to wait.

I have zero experience with medical situations. I often joke that I purposely chose a career that is the exact opposite of a medical professional for a reason. Even listening to someone talk about someone bleeding turns my stomach. In addition, I hadn't witnessed anyone in my family, since my Grandpa died when I was 15, hospitalized for a significant amount of time. Needless to say, I was out of practice. My mind was still telling me, "This will be fine. This will end fine. He is where people are healed."

Exactly 29 minutes later, I received another call from the same doctor. He sounded different. He delivered his next words with urgency.

"Your husband coded. He is presently having CPR performed on him."

I am now aware of the seriousness of his situation, I am also fully awake.

In the next 5 or 6 minutes, I changed out of my pajamas, threw on pants and a hoodie, redid my messy ponytail that had become unrecognizable in the night, and called my mother-in-law. None of the kids were up yet. It was, after all, just past 6:30 am.

My mother-in-law answered immediately. I had already texted her that her son was in the ICU, so she picked up after the first ring. I was crying before I delivered the news.

In just the 5 minutes after the call from the doctor, my husband could already be gone, or possibly he's still alive. That spectrum terrified me. The difference was devastation versus hope. Debby heard the tears in my voice.

"I have to go to the hospital. Can you come watch the kids?"

Before I left, I went into my oldest child's room. Lincoln was slightly awake, having heard me on the phone. The unusual occurrence had awoken him.

"Daddy's in the ICU. I have to go to the hospital. Grandma's on her way."

"Okay." he nodded his still sleepy head. Lincoln was already aware that Daddy had suffered blood clots in his legs and his lungs. My husband had been on a blood thinner drip all week. As soon as I left, Lincoln started researching. He later told me that that's how he gets through traumatic times. Gaining as much information as he can about the circumstances soothes him.

I left before my mother in law arrived, banking on the hope that no one would wake up in the ten minutes between me leaving, and her arriving. She lives literally a mile and a half away.

Unbeknownst to me, at some point following the phone call to my mother-in-law and my drive to the hospital, Scott's emergency hit social media. I was 5 minutes from my house, pulling onto highway 34 when my friend Heather called me.

Just seeing her name on my screen, I answered the phone crying. Crying in front of people has always been something I have avoided at all costs. Crying on the phone to someone falls under that rule, but this is Heather. She is one of my closest friends. Her heart is purely loving, and I know that she won't judge me and will only want to help. She confessed to me later on that she was not crying until after she heard my tearful "Hello" upon answering her call.

"Ang! What's going on with Scott?"

I fill her in. I've got 30 more minutes to drive so I spill what I know so far, which isn't much, including whether or not my husband is even still alive. For some reason, I didn't think to call the hospital to check. The first of many mind slips in the coming weeks. I suspect that my brain was beginning a protective phase.

As I talk, she consoles me, listens, and relays information to her husband, also a Scott, and also one of my and my husband's closest friends.

We met Scott and Heather through mutual friends. They had middle and elementary school girls, Carly and Courtney, and I had a 4 week old at the time. My kids and I call them by their full names for some reason. So Scott is Scottbingham, and Heather is Heatherbingham. We nicknamed their youngest daughter, Coco because it was easier for our smallest kiddos than saying, Courtney. Even though my kids are now perfectly capable of saying Courtney, they still call her Coco. They adore her and her sister and so do I.

Their kids are grown now and mine are still small, so our paths don't cross like they used to, but we built a house less than a mile away, and living so close to them was a major selling point for us. I was thankful that the first person I spoke with at the beginning of this hand we'd been dealt was Heather. We would talk daily over the next month.

After disconnecting with Heather, my mind got to work. I had no control over the thoughts that began rolling in. The "If he's dead, I need to be prepared" thoughts.

My mind was in "Expect the best, but prepare for the worst," mode.

I began thinking about our life insurance policy. Mine is excellent. If I die, he and the kids are set. I'm healthy, relatively young, no past medical issues to speak of beside a handful of knee surgeries and a bunch of pregnancies.

On the other hand, Scott's life insurance would only tide us over for a while. He's always been overweight, and that alone kept his takeaway numbers lower than the ideal.

I began thinking of what new career I could do. I've maxed out any hope of an increase in pay at my job. Despite the glamorous perception of a radio broadcaster, small-town radio won't make you rich. My husband's salary nearly doubles mine. He extended himself into sales which helped that. As a homeschooling mom, I only have so many hours in the day, so plain old broadcaster is about as far as I can extend myself. Even that keeps me hopping.

Law Enforcement? I thought. Nope, I'd have to be away from the kids too long. I know lots of people that would probably hire me in a second. Going back to school is an option but it would have to be a quick program so I could get right onto a money-making career. I'll move in with my brother! He lives in Nebraska. This seemed like the best option, but the thought was quickly derailed by "Jesus! I'm 44 years old and my husband might not be around anymore." These back and forth thoughts sent me spiraling, bouncing back and forth between,

Please, God! Let my husband be okay!" to, "I need to make plans in case he isn't. "

I don't remember my arrival at the hospital. It's Friday, it's early, there's not much activity so I got a great parking space. I ran to the entrance, and flew through the main doors.

Finding the right words is important to me, but I wasn't sure how to explain to the reception staff what I needed. My face gave away a lot, and they instinctively lead me through it.

In the movies, someone runs into the hospital, frantically asks for the patient, and runs down the hallway toward the room, only to be stopped by a doctor who says, "You can't go in there." The person then fights the restraining grip of the doctor, and screams something over his shoulder, then gives in, only to be escorted to the waiting room where they then, wait. Wait for news, good or bad. I can usually tell from the tone of the music, or from the last interaction the patient and character had what kind of news they'll receive.

Even though I'm now in a movie (this can't possibly be really happening) it was nothing like that. Reception was confused about my wanting to go to the ICU. I had been told to "get here now!" I assumed they'd have my name and description and give me instructions on how to get to ICU, their voices yelling "Elevator B..." as I ran off. As I said, I've never experienced anything like this.

They are unsure why I think I'm permitted in the ICU. I still don't know if my husband has been resuscitated. I think to myself, "Please, someone just tell me he's okay."

The young woman at the front greeter desk (who I will see often in the following weeks and who tells me later that I broke her heart that morning) calls ICU. She explains that the patient in 2006's wife is here. A few "sure's, mkays, and uh huh's later, she hangs up the phone.

"Someone will call me when you can come up. The waiting room is closed, but you can have a seat right over there." She looks down for a moment.

"Oh, and he's stable."

I think I crumbled with relief into the chair directly outside the "closed for covid" waiting room.

Of course he is. He couldn't be anything else. Certainly not the alternative in my head. Processing the previous hour is difficult, so I just don't. Not my choice. My brain, I believe is now protecting me from the trauma of it all.

Chapter 2

Roughly 10 minutes later, Scott's sister and his Dad arrived. They had driven over together to meet me. We are about to learn just how tricky the hospital restrictions are as a result of Covid.

It's not what you know, but who you know, and Julie knew someone. Scott's sister had called ahead to her friend, Paula. Paula is the head nurse on the ICU floor and by the grace of God, she was working that morning. Julie and Paula had met through their daughters' sports. I was about to meet Paula.

Paula had our back. It was like having an escort through the unknown. She gently answered all of my questions, as though she'd done this before or something. She explained that we couldn't see him until 8 am but she would try to see if we could go in at 7:30.

She filled me in on what had happened while we watched the clock tick-tick-tick. I was about to learn the definition of words that had never been said to me.

Scott had suffered a pulmonary embolism. The blood clot in his lung had blocked the artery between his heart and his lung. This resulted in cardiac arrest. Scott's heart stopped from the stress. He coded. Someone among the nurses and doctors who were caring for him in the ICU performed CPR. I was not able to find out who, or a definite answer on "how long." The image in my mind is one of these fit medical professionals leaping on top of Scott, and pounding chest compressions until the monitor stopped its dull high pitched continuous tone, and instead began to beep.

Once he was resuscitated, he was intubated, or placed on life support. A tube was inserted into his lung designed to breathe for him. This is how I would soon find him.

Despite restrictions of one person in the ICU room allowed, the severity of the situation justified a little rule-breaking. Although we were there to see him, we could also be there to see him for the last time.

Julie, John, and I talked. I'm afraid I can't tell you about what. I truly don't remember. I know we were all in and out of tears. Paula brought us all some coffee as if this head nurse supervisor was a server in a restaurant. I took notice of her compassion. It felt honest.

"I think you know someone I know." she said.

Intrigued and eager for a subject change, I inquired. It turns out this world is incredibly small. She grew up with a gentleman that my husband and I had met in Memphis Tennessee at the annual Country Cares Seminar for St. Jude Children's Research Hospital. His name is Dave Marsh. He grew up in Missouri...so did she. We met Dave in Memphis, we live in Oregon, now so does Paula. Dave was a radio broadcaster too, and his station did fundraiser for St. Jude like ours. Scott and I hit it off with Dave immediately, and several years in a row, he vacationed at our home. Paula, the nursing supervisor who is serving me coffee and keeping me informed on my husband's medical situation, ran around with Dave when they were teens. And here, the two of us, meeting for the first time, are making that connection.

Time passed, and we settled into the waiting, watching every tick of the clock. Already though, at this early hour as our community began preparing for their Friday workday, I was receiving messages of curiosity, love, and support. I had not yet shared an announcement on social media, the fastest way to spread information wildfire. The details known to others at this point were that prayers were needed and the situation was dire. A friend named Heather Paris was the first to reach out. She sent me 10 dollars to get coffee. With time on my hands still, I quickly messaged her back to tell her how much I appreciated her gesture, and that she was the first to think of such a gift. I couldn't have known that over the next 12 hours, an army would deploy on my behalf, comprised of individual soldiers unaware that others, too had joined the battle.

Nearly 7:30 now, Paula returned.

"There's something for you down in the E.R.," she said.

"Something?" I wasn't sure what in the world could have been delivered to the E.R. I had only been there less than an hour.

"Okay," I stammered, and got to my feet, headed to the first floor.

Dumbfounded and unable to imagine what I would possibly find, I robotically exited the elevator, and pushed through the door to the E.R.

Chapter 3

My "something," was instead, someone. Cowboy!

I ran to him, and he embraced me. His flack vest was obvious as I fell into him.

Chris is a Linn County Sheriff's deputy and a great friend of Scott's and mine. He had heard of our situation on social media and drove immediately...to the wrong hospital. He was under the impression that Scott was at Lebanon hospital, unaware that Scott had been transferred to Corvallis a week prior. I hadn't made a big deal out of Scott's hospitalization and didn't even share it with close friends, imagining it would be something that would come up over cocktails down the road. "So Scott went to the hospital in December," "What!? No!" "What happened?" "Is he feeling better now?" Something along those lines.

I sobbed to Cowboy, forgetting again that I don't cry in front of people as a rule.

He explained to me that he had been on patrol, heard about Scott, headed to Lebanon, realized his error, and drove 45 minutes back to Corvallis. He still beat everyone else to me.

"Can I pray with you?" he asked me?

"Yes!"

"Dear Heavenly Father, (insert the most perfect prayer here). I can't tell you his exact words, but his background as a loving 7th Day Adventist, father, husband, grandfather, and law enforcement officer gifted him the perfect words of healing for my husband, and strength for me.

I explained the events of the prior week, and how I had mistakenly believed this was a routine minor medical emergency that would resolve itself with proper treatment and medication. I shared the phone calls that I had received that morning, and all the details up to the point where I burst through the E.R. exit door into the lobby into Cowboy's arms.

Cowboy and Scott met like many of his friendships began, playing softball. Cowboy is a couple of years older than Scott. I met him as a result of my husband's friendship with him. Often we would all play golf, or Cowboy would stop by while on patrol just to say hey. Our family supports our law enforcement officers in any way we can so we might give him lunch, or a soda, or water, or just company to help him through his day.

He and his wife, Vonda have always been close with our family. They've seen our kids grow, and even spent holidays with us. Now, here he stood in the E.R Lobby, my first uniformed soldier to show up. He now had my tears on his uniform. 4 days later, I was able to share his kindness with everyone.

Facebook Post from December 21st.

We haven't been alone once in any moment of this and our entire family is basking in your love. I outsourced a number of housekeeping tasks today. Trying to Julie Tatum and Debby Childers a break from being my go-tos. They are hurting too and still worried about me

All requests were met with speedy, joyful acceptance today. I started to list them all but there was seriously so much help today, and over the three days before that, I fear I'd leave someone out and I'd feel like an ass. Plus so many have taken it upon themselves to show their support in their own unique ways. My favorite way to thank you is in person with handwritten, tear-stained thank you cards a close second. I also opened a number of well-wishing cards and witnessing even more generosity

The parking lot is full here, and so are the beds so it seems many are bailing water out and lowering the dingys from this same boat. I'm aware that others' outcomes haven't progressed as well as ours. I'm grateful to be able to share so much good news and know we've been blessed.

Friday morning, right after I arrived and before I knew Scott's condition after he coded, I was told by one of the nurses that there was "something" for me in the e.r. I was clueless so I left the waiting i.c.u area and went downstairs. When I opened the door, there stood Chris

Fairchild. He was " something indeed. " in his Linn County sheriff's deputy uniform. I nearly knocked him over in a hug and got snot and tears all over him. He asked if he could pray with me. Then he held me up and prayed. He had first gone to Lebanon only to find out Scott was in Corvallis, then blazed back on over to comfort me. I'm not sure if I'll ever be able to retell that story outloud without sobbing, so I thought I'd share it here. I was trying to be present throughout these knowing I would want to reflect on each one and more importantly, share the numerous, divine experiences with Scott Schuler and everyone who loves him.

Chapter 4

As I returned to the "closed for Covid" waiting room, I was told that we were now able to step into the Intensive Care Unit. The last time that I had been in an ICU when I was 15. My grandpa, "Poppy," had a heart attack at Portland airport before leaving for a vacation with my mom, dad, and my grandma, "Granny." He was taken to the hospital, placed on life support, and passed away soon after. I was able to visit him one last time...in the ICU.

A pair of double doors opened after we checked in by phone. I remember picking up the phone, and not knowing what to say.

"I'm here for, Scott Schuler." stumbled out.

"Come on back."

John and I walked down a long, wide hallway to see his son. The ICU rooms were on the left. Each room was occupied, although I wouldn't notice until I walked that long mile out sometime later. Scott's room was directly ahead of the double entry doors and had a gorgeous view of the hospital campus. Probably more for my benefit than his at this point.

He looked like he was sleeping, even with the tubes. At home, he wears a BiPAP machine. I jokingly call it his "life support."

At this point, I'm the reluctant star in a movie. This isn't real, and won't feel real for some time. I'm watching another woman walk into an ICU room to see her husband.

The tube was doing the breathing for him. Nathan was the nurse on duty and he was typing when I entered. With my emotions on high and surface level, I took my husband's hand and cried.

John was with me. Julie had offered to stay back in the "closed for covid" waiting room so that he could see Scott.

I'm certain that I could be friends with nearly everyone I met in the ICU, including Nathan. Something he said that morning will never leave me.

Marriage is hard. Scott and I have been struggling with ours for years. More so, I've been struggling. He seems to be just fine with the status quo. But while I've spent my years trying to be the best version of myself, he began drinking heavily and putting on a large amount of weight.

He's always been a large man. 6 foot 6, and 350 when we met. He got down under 300 when I was pregnant with our first daughter. Most recently, I knew that he was over 400 pounds, and my best guess was significantly over 400 pounds. We had purchased a scale that went up to 450, and he was unable to weigh in on it. That's how I knew.

When we married, I had purchased him 3 x tall shirts for birthdays and holidays. He was now ordering 5x tall on Amazon. None of this mattered upon seeing him on life support and knowing that he almost spent his final week on earth in a hospital, leaving behind his 5 children, the youngest of which is only 4 years old.

Nathan and I had made medical small talk, I think. I don't remember much, but I know I expressed how angry I had been at my husband's life choices that may have helped put him where he is now. I think I must have also expressed that I had tried everything I knew to prevent it. Nathan took this opportunity and said, "That's why married men live longer than single men."

Grateful for an opening, I questioned, "Really?"

Nathan looked up from his typing and replied, "I certainly think so. I'm always hesitant to send these little old men home from here knowing that there's no one at home to take care of them. They don't make it long."

Knowing he's an expert in this subject, I didn't doubt his assessment. I now think of this often. Maybe I'm here, at this moment in the ICU with my husband, who I chose to marry, and have a family with, but who I haven't been very fond of in recent years, just to nag him into recovery. Maybe this is my path for a necessary lesson to further awaken in life.

John held his son's hand. How strange and awful that must be, I thought. To be in one's upper 70's, and see your child on life support. He may have cried. My eyes were too blurry to know. He tagged in Scott's sister Julie soon after, perhaps seeing his son in such condition was too much. It would be for any parent.

Julie and I held Scott's hands. Scott was her rock growing up. Her father figure when their Dad, a Vietnam War Veteran was not available. This had to be so hard on her, harder than I could imagine.

I've pieced together to next days from notes that I took. I was on a roller coaster of emotions from being grateful for the tsunami of love and support from friends and family (not yet the community at this point...they weren't yet aware of what was going on with their beloved morning show host) to devastating, worst-case scenario thoughts of my family's future.

As word got out, I began receiving messages. Supportive, kind, loving messages that sustained me in the first hours. Messages from my husband's friends that I barely knew, and messages from people that we had helped over the years who were now there for me.

At half-past noon, Day 1:

Angela, I don't even know where to start. You and Scott have supported me and my family through some of the scariest and darkest points in our lives. From supporting our open heart benefit to supporting/showering us with love when the car came through the house, you guys have impacted and changed our lives a few different times. Your family has a very special place in our hearts, so when I read your post, my heart sank. I can't imagine how scary, stressful, and exhausting these last few weeks have been. Your strength reminds me of my wife Michelle. She kept everyone up to date during my surgeries, kept the house running, took care of the kids, and the million other things that still needed to be done, so I could rest and recover. However, what she didn't tell me was how scared she was and how exhausting it was trying to keep everything together, and stay positive for the kids. I see you. You will be on our hearts and on minds. I pray you get rest. I pray you get moments of joy amongst the storm. I pray you get time to cry, and grieve, and scream. I pray for strength. I pray for peace. I pray for protection. I pray you get reminded daily how much God loves you, how much he is delighted in you, and how faithful he is, even in this. If there is anything we can do to support you guys, please let us know. We absolutely adore your family. Be well, friend.

I must have read and re-read this message a dozen times or more that first day. The words from this man dove deep within me, and I couldn't find the words to respond, although I tried.

Dan is an extremely talented musician. Our paths crossed over the years but not consistently. He performed in some competitions that our radio station hosted for musicians, and often placed quite high. He has a soft, lovely, soulful voice, and I have always rooted for him to find his way in music over the years. Like many musicians, he has a family to support, so a steady job outside of music took priority for Dan. I hadn't spoken to him in years when I received this message. Our interactions before this had been me encouraging him. Dan's message made me well aware that I was in a new world now.

I began to see that God was not only involved now, He had been involved for years, decades maybe, preparing me for this and building an army for me. God put individuals in my path over the years that were now showing up, out of the trees, armed with love. Foolishly, I had always thought that God had put me in their path to help and support them. Although fear crept in often over the coming days, it was also often quickly snuffed out by one of my soldiers.

Chapter 5

I held his hand, I answered texts, I watched his chest go up and down, and I watched his vitals (which I still didn't understand.) I made arrangements, I didn't eat, and I prayed.

I've always prayed. My conversations with God are generally expressions of gratitude. Gratitude for the beautiful day spent with my children, the ability to homeschool, my health, my job, my home, etc. I pray for others' desires but consciously try not to ask for anything. One exception is that I ask that he protect my children and keep them safe from harm and illness. I am spiritual, but not well versed in worship. There have been too many divine moments in my life for me to deny that God is in everything. He walks with me, and somehow with everyone else at the same time.

In discussions with my friends, God is mentioned in passing, but not generally the center of the conversation. This left me unaware of which of my friends I could openly praise Him with. Turns out, all of them. Once again, I have been a fool.

Just before 1 pm, Day 1:

I just got to Chicago with my daughter, this isn't the news anyone would want to see. I've been praying and will continue to pray. I'm sorry you're going through this. But I am praying!! For him and you. You're his lifeline. You're there to speak the words into existence. Words of life, healing and hope. I already prayed the Lord will lead you to the right words to speak and pray over him. The power of life and death is in the tongue. I know it's tough but speak it into existence. I'm in agreement with you. What can I do to help you? I may not be in Oregon but I can organize almost anything from anywhere? Do you need meals delivered to the kids? Groceries? Please let me know. You know you have a tribe! Sending YOU and Scottie my love and sincere prayers.-Amber Morelli

Amber and Scott attended high school together. I may have met her at one of his high school reunions. I know I've met her on more than one occasion. She is a bold, alpha female, and I liked her immediately.

The right words did come. I did write down scripture. I did everything she said at a time when I didn't know what else to do. I looked up scripture about life, health, fear, and the right ones came to me. I've only just stepped into this alternate reality. Just hours prior, I was planning Christmas, excitement, and joy. The whiplash from the jolted alternate course left me still in shock.

I couldn't do this on my own.

Earlier in the week, my friend, Heidi had given me a Christmas gift. It was a mug, a pen, and a notepad for things like a grocery list. The notepad was in my purse still along with the pen. It was paper, so I wrote on it.

Jeremiah 17:14

Heel me O Lord and I shall be healed; save me and I shall be saved for thou art my praise

Fear thou not for I am with Thee

I am the Lord that heel thee

And I will take sickness away from the midst of thee

A merry heart doeth good like a medicine

Keep the heart with all diligence

But let patience have her perfect work that ye may be perfect and entire wanting nothing

Let not your heart be troubled neither let it be afraid

Jesus, I strive to walk in the path of the righteous person. Walk with me in my life that I may have your peace and healing

I recognize my handwriting, but the words were all new to me. They gave me what I needed...hope.

All-day, I sat by my husband's bedside. His birthday would be the next day. He would be 49. I wrote scripture, answered messages as the news was starting to leak out, gave updates, held it together, and lost it.

I repeated this cycle all day. There was nothing else to do. I was useless. His life was in the hands of medical professionals.

I make it a point to stay busy. If I'm not doing something, something isn't getting done. As my husband's "caregiver," I was like royalty, or at least, like an employee. Permitted in his room, I was welcome at all hours, but with him on life support, all I could do was pray, so I did. Like it was my job.

I can't imagine working in that environment, seeing people at their absolute lowest point. I had no control over when the tears would flow. Most of the time, it was one thought in particular that got them flowing.

Our 4-year-old daughter still sleeps in our bed. I'll confess, I love it. I built a platform for her toddler bed to raise it to our king bed's level. I transfer her over to her bed, but ultimately, she crawls back over to me every night. We lie down together to go to sleep each evening. Before drifting off, she crawls over to Daddy and asks him to tell her the story of the Three Little Pigs. He has a special way of telling it. We have a book that we've read to all of our kids with the story. There are many variations of the story, and one we tell has a lot of humor. He never says "no" when she asks, no matter how tired he is. He's been in the hospital for more than a week now, and she hasn't had him home to tell the story. After the first night, she dragged out the audio CD that came with the book, found her CD player, and walked around our house playing the story. I kept thinking of this, and without fail, bawled every single time. Now she doesn't have her Daddy, and I'm not there with her either. She's 4. Will she even remember that he told her the story if he never gets to tell it again? I'm telling ya, Niagra Falls, every time.

So as I sat by his bed feeling moments of having it all together, and clear-headed. That thought would destroy me over and over all day.

Meanwhile, wheels that I was not aware of were in motion. I was told that my neighbors, the Gillotts would be delivering their luxury

RV to the Pastega House for me to be able to stay at the hospital. This generous gift would save me from having to drive home 35 miles and back each day...at least while Scott's condition was touch and go. I had already planned to stay this night and all nights until...whenever.

Facebook post-December 17th at 10:11 am

I feel the need to update all of my husband's fans. He is stable but in icu in Corvallis. 2 Mondays ago, he had a bout with atrial fibrillation. Lebanon e.r. was able to right the rhythm, he came home and took it easy for a couple days, went back to work but was having shortness of breath. Tuesday he went back to the e.r. after consulting with his doctor who suspected blood clots. That was confirmed and he was admitted Tuesday night in Corvallis. They've been administering blood thinners via i.v all week. We've been waiting for the medicine to work to dissolve the clots. This morning, the doctor called to tell me that he'd woken up extremely short of breath with an accelerated heart rate. He was taken to i.c.u for a more powerful blood thinner and intubated. I received another call roughly 30 minutes later that his heart had stopped and they were at present administering CPR. I made the 100-year drive to Corvallis and finally learned that he was stabilized but was without oxygen for a significant time. Fortunately, though, he was in ICU when that happened so action was taken immediately. He is in excellent hands and I know of the massive amount of prayers and love directed at him. The kids are in good hands too. Anyone that wants to pop in though, I know they love the visits. Thank you to everyone that has reached out. I will certainly keep you updated. I may reach out to friends in Corvallis for use of your shower

The responses blessed me. I run in a circle with some individuals who are experts in prayer. I've always felt that some people have a direct link to God, and he listens to their prayers in particular. They've got God on their side. Not that the rest of us don't, of course, we do too. Without a doubt, I can say that the immediate prayers for healing for Scott, and strength for me and the kids were enormously powerful.

Tyra Thompson Parillo

Oh no! I'm so sorry Angela I'm for your husband and your family.
Dear Heavenly Father,

I trust in Your power and grace that will sustain and restore Scott. Loving Father, touch him now with Your healing hands, for I believe that Your will is for him to be well in mind, body, soul and spirit. Cover him with the Most Precious Blood of Your Son, our Lord Jesus Christ, from the top of his head to the soles of his feet. Amen

Responses were of concern, assistance, and shock.

Ron Sapp

I am praying.... The last time I was praying for him he was in the hospital with an ear bit off... just like then I am believing for a full recovery.... I love all of you!

As a child, my husband had been trampled by a horse. He was 6 years old and the horse belonged to a neighbor. As the oft-told story goes, the horse had been mistreated by the neighbor boys. At 6 years old with a family of farmers, Scott only knew horses to be gentle. He entered the field to feed the horse when it knocked him to the ground, stepped on his back, and bit off a significant piece of his ear. He was rushed to the hospital where doctors lamented the fact that they didn't have the piece to reattach. Scott's dad, John, and his Uncle Don went back to the field on the hunt. They combed the field until they located the ear, threw it on ice, and raced back to the hospital. Doctors attempted to reattach the ear. It didn't take, and from that day on, he only had a partial left ear. The first time I met him, the night he trained me at the radio station on the night shift, with his left side toward me, my first thought was, "What the heck is wrong with his ear!?"

Ron, like many others, would reach out over the coming weeks to check on me, get updates on Scott, and find out exactly what to pray for. As I said, in my circle the spirit is abundant. If one were to hire prayers to make things happen this is the group.

Chapter 6

I took a break for the first time when the RV arrived. Julie was there to give me the tour, as she had spoken with the owners that had generously loaned it to me.

Scott and I had done numerous fundraisers over the years for the Pastega House. We had partnered up in golf tournaments hosted by the local Pepsi delivery service. My golf bag is a Pepsi bag that I won at a tournament several years ago. It's a wonderful facility that provides a place to stay for people who have a loved one in the hospital but live a significant distance away. There are lovely hotel-like rooms for guests as well as RV spots for those who wish to stay in their own space. Thankfully I lived just a smidge over the distance threshold and was approved for an RV space.

Laura and Dave Gillott are not "Tell us how we can help you" kind of people. They are "Here's how we can help you, we'll be right over" kind of people. They drove their luxury RV over, set it up, cleaned it and left before I could thank them. Their home is 100 yards from mine as the crow flies. We attended a concert in her front yard last summer that was one of the best I've been to. I love a laid-back atmosphere where kids can run around, and adults can enjoy live music, but still chat if they want. Country singer, Matt Stillwell had performed. He pulled in with his trailer transformer. It's a trailer that transforms into a stage. I helped him set up his merchandise, chatted with my neighbors, and friends and drove less than a mile back to my house when it was over.

At one point during the night, I stood in a circle with Dave and listened to some chatter. I shook hands with Laura and thanked her for the evening. That was about it.

Laura is an accomplished and well-known real estate agent in our community, but she's known nationwide. She is the definition of a successful businesswoman. I often wonder how it began for her. I would love for her to write the story of her success.

My husband has recorded commercials for Laura's company for quite some time. His relationship with them goes deeper than mine. Yet, they entrusted me with their RV, no questions asked. I never even spoke to them...it was just there.

Julie told me that Laura had gone around inside, cleaning the RV before I arrived. I wish she hadn't. I would have loved the distraction of wiping it down myself. It was a beautiful, deep red motorhome, almost a tour bus.

I was told that there were clothes in the closet, towels in the bathroom, and food throughout the RV that I was welcome to, and to please eat as much as I could. Laura and Dave were watching what they eat, and they were hoping to be rid of the junk food. I hadn't had much of an appetite, and wouldn't for quite a while.

A shower though, that was heaven. I used shampoo and conditioner that I found in the small RV bathroom. The towel was just so perfectly rough and absorbent. I found a hairdryer and was able to make myself somewhat presentable.

I threw some snacks in my purse in case my appetite ever came back. Snacks that I could eat without any prep. A granola bar and some beef jerky would likely be my dinner.

From the Pastega House to the Hospital, the drive was roughly a quarter of a mile. Had my husband been admitted in the summer, I would have walked. December in Oregon, however, is yucky. Grey, damp, gloomy, depressing. I drove.

Arriving once again at the double doors to the ICU, I still wasn't sure how to announce myself.

"Front desk."

"Hi, um Angela for Sc...."

"Come on back."

Nothing had changed. A machine still breathed for him. His eyes remained closed, and I wondered if I was here to spend his last moments with him.

At the same time, my friend, Staci was in a building next door with her husband, PJ. PJ, another high school buddy of Scott's, had an appointment at the cancer center. Staci sent me a text.

Staci Stitzel: Weird just over heard a patient talking to one of the receptionists about Scott at PJ's appointment.

She didn't recognize the woman but said that she was about my mother in law's age. I asked what the woman had said.

Staci: She said hes over at the hospital has been there for a few days not doing well, he is on life support.

My friend Lauren, a nurse, was in town for her son's basketball game at West Albany. She had overheard another parent in the bleachers talking about Scott and texted me in a panic. It became clear that Scott was on the minds of people in our community. I started to feel like a liaison between his condition and their concern, and I took it very seriously. This wasn't just town gossip. This man is important to more than just our little family.

Staci offered to take me to dinner but understood if I wanted to stay with Scott. Going against that desire, I took her up on her offer.

Staci: Okay, we will be there in about 20.

PJ and Staci took me to their favorite Mexican restaurant in Corvallis. The place was packed, but we found a table in the back. We had talked the entire car ride and the conversation continued through dinner. It wasn't entirely about the turn of events that day, or Scott's health. We caught up on everything. They had recently put down their beloved dog, Tank. We talked of how difficult that was. PJ's health was also a subject. I felt in a bit of a daze, but did my best to stay present with my friends. Part of me was thankful for dinner with friends, but part of me also realized the reason behind them asking me to dinner, and the two realities resisted each other. I was also growing very, very tired and struggled to stay focused through that.

Our food took longer than expected, so the night ran long. I had received a message from my friend, Angie that she and her husband, Alva would be coming by the RV that evening with some supplies for me. We agreed on a time to meet but I was cutting it close.

Here I was, my friend PJ, coming from an appointment at the cancer center, and now buying me dinner, and my friend Angie with a quadriplegic child that requires 24/7 care, bringing me supplies. I struggled to feel worthy of these exceptional friends of mine.

Chapter 7

PJ and Staci dropped me off at the RV, and hugged me goodbye. Angie and Alva arrived at the RV shortly after I did. Perhaps around 8 o clock. Angie has trouble with her knees and had difficulty climbing the stairs into the tour bus. Alva and I helped her. She is only a few years older than me but has suffered tremendous losses in her life and her health has suffered as a result.

I believe I met Angie when she reached out to me at the radio station to promote a fundraiser. Her first child, AJ had passed away at roughly 4 months old. He had been born premature. Each year, she organized a fundraiser on his birthday for Children's Miracle Network. She was profoundly grateful to them for their gift of time she was able to have with her AJ. She founded AJ's Angels and hoped to raise enough money to have something named for AJ at the hospital.

She has 2 other children. Michael, and McKenzie. My daughter, Sunny became fast friends with McKenzie when they were smaller. McKenzie was a spunky little thing, full of energy and life. Just before she turned 7, she contracted Entero Virus. The virus resulted in devastating paralysis. I was pregnant with Braddock when the ordeal began. I kept in contact with Angie as she took McKenzie to the hospital to try to figure out what was going on. In the coming days, McKenzie lost all ability to move, and even to breathe. The damage was permanent, and McKenzie is a quadriplegic. She recently turned 13. Confined to her bed, she and Sunny have remained friends. They communicate through their tablets and play games online together. I have made it a point to help Angie and Alva provide as good a life as possible for McKenzie. Whatever they need, Scott and I try to provide. They got a raw deal, and need a true team of supporters to get through each day. Angie will go days without significant sleep when nursing is sparse and it all falls to her. Alva is the breadwinner and works extra hours as often as possible to help make ends meet. McKenzie's needs are extensive and expensive, and only some of it is covered by their insurance. Yet somehow, Angie maintains the energy to fiercely fight on McKenzie's behalf. She is a kind and loving friend and always remembers my kids, all dang 5 of them, on their birthdays.

She and Alva came in lugging an enormous Ikea bag full of supplies for me. They had either gone shopping, or cleaned out their pantry, or both. They had anticipated everything I might need throughout my stay, the length of which was yet to be determined.

The two of them sat on the couch opposite the sleeper sofa that would be my bed later that night. Angie took each item out of the bag explaining her thought behind including it in my care package. The distraction was welcome. I was exhausted emotionally, but thankful to have something else to think about and talk about. I think Angie knew this was what I needed.

She also had the presence of mind to include a journal and a pen. Her experience with hospital stays was invaluable in this situation. An expert of sorts, she often knows more than the medical professionals who care for McKenzie. She may not be an expert in medicine in general, but she is an expert in her daughter's care. It's quite impressive. She provided me with helpful advice throughout our conversation. The journal, she suggested would help me keep track of his Doctors, nurses, medications, and any questions that may arise when there was no one to ask. That journal became a priceless prop in our journey and will reemerge over and over throughout this story.

Also in the enormous blue Ikea bag, every comfort food you can imagine, from cup o noodles, granola bars, beef sticks, cheese, potato chips and even a six-pack of hard ciders. Alva's idea. I didn't end up drinking any but appreciated his thoughtfulness.

They stayed late, past 10 pm. Angie can talk! I often have to budget a couple of hours when I visit, knowing she'll have a lot to say. I love being a shoulder for her and letting her bounce her frustrations off of me. She's a remarkable lady and I'm in awe of all she finds the energy to do for McKenzie and her family. Naturally, she doesn't think she does enough, and here she was, being a shoulder for me, letting me bounce my frustrations off of her, distracting me from my racing, worst-case scenario thoughts with her hopefulness and relatable stories. Alva is a funny man. He even made me laugh several times that night. When they left, I said a tiny prayer of gratitude for bringing them into my life.

After my friends left, I decided to bring this day to an end and find a way to sleep. Angie had stopped at the store upon my request to get me a bottle of Benadryl. I knew I would need assistance to shut my mind off for at least a couple of hours of sleep.

The journal that Angie and Alva gave to me in the blue Ikea bag of goodies would prove to be a Godsend. I began writing that very night.

Nurse ? 10:18 said you gripped her with your right hand but not your left.

ICU phone number 541-768-5126

Room 2006

Pin # 1757

I'm alone tonight in Laura Gillott's RV. It's beautiful. I don't know how anything works. I was counting on this being one and done-you get well, you get home. I think you downplayed this to me all week. I'm not mad. Not anymore. Now I just want you well.

The planet is praying I swear, everyone! It's pretty amazing, really, how loved you are. I think about that sometimes when I'm really struggling to love you-That out of everyone on the planet, you picked me to make a life with.

A lot of it has been fun. You took this broken girl and decided she was worth the effort. I can't be easy to love. Always looking, searching for whatever it is I'm missing. It feels good to cry. I've wanted to-all the time so many days. But the kids were around, or something else. Releasing that feels good. I wiped 2 tears from your eye today. During the moments you woke up and fought your situation, a tear fell. I don't know if it's fear, or emotion. I wiped it and told you it was ok, and that you are going to be okay. I made a list of things I want to hear from the doctors. My mind is very good at playing out worst case scenarios, and believing it to be real, so I needed something else for it to focus on.

1. I wanted to hear that you were stabilized.
2. Brain activity is good
3. Clots are breaking up/dissolved
4. Medicine is working
5. His body is responding
6. He's waking up
7. He's asking for you
8. Your voice
9. He can go home now

It's an hour and a half until your birthday. I got you a patio umbrella with L.E.D. lights for over the hot tub. I was going to assemble it today.

I really want our kids to have their dad. They really love you a lot. Poor Sunny. She's so worried about you. I am here away from them but I want so bad to comfort them.

I'm going to come see you at 6. I'll have to get coffee first. I love you.

11:26 pm, day 1

I'm thinking of things you do that I don't give you credit for

1. RV stuff. Knowing how to get things working and how to fix things when they aren't working.

A large, walk-around queen size bed was at the back of the vehicle. In the front, a couch that turned into a hide-a-bed. I chose to sleep in the main living space on the hide-a-bed. Try as we might, Julie and I couldn't figure out the thermostat earlier in the day. Unwilling to trouble the Gillotts with questions, I slept in my clothes and bundled up. I didn't expect sleep to come easily, or at all even. Despite having had an exhausting day. I slept some but it was shallow, and riddled with dreams.

After just a few hours, I awoke to the unknown. Already in my clothes from the day before, and having had a shower, I washed my face, and brushed my teeth. Feeling the need to redeem myself for my appearance the previous day, I threw my hair into a french braid. A baseball hat with "Ketchikan" on it completed my "going to the ICU" look. I borrowed this from Dave Gillott's RV closet. They said I could use anything. Before I left, I snapped a selfie in the cap and sent it to Dave, knowing that me making myself at home would please them. It would me, if I were them. Again, I grabbed the journal and pen.

7:21 am 12-18.21

I wonder what time you were born. I'll ask your mom.

Happy Birthday

You are still taking a long winter's nap.

Nurse Liz says you have a temperature, but it's coming down. I've got to remember to breathe today.

"He Healeth the broken."

"The tongue of the wise is health."

"A faithful ambassador is health."

Jeremiah 17:14

Heal me O Lord and I shall be healed; save me and I shall be saved for thou art my praise

Fear thou not for I am with thee

I am the Lord that healeth thee

And I will take sickness away from the midst of thee.

Alisa is your respiratory nurse-expert this morning.

God is in control

A merry heart doeth good like a medicine.

Keep the heart with all diligence.

But let patience have her perfect work that ye may be perfect and entire wanting nothing.

Let not your heart be troubled neither let it be afraid.

Jesus I strive to walk in the path of the righteous person . Walk with me in my life that I may have your peace and healing.

Veronica is your nurse this morning.

Dr. Young, a resident is your doctor this morning.

Dr. Delmonico was yesterday.

Dr. Talbot is the doctor that called me yesterday.

Alva and Angie brought oodles of supplies last night and stayed and chatted until after 10 p. It was nice and kept my mind busy.

Alva has lost 60 pounds. He quit drinking 3 years ago.

Alva works here in Plant engineering.

Prototonix medication

Brushing your teeth this morning

X rays @ 8:30

No change. My husband remained in his ICU bed, on life support. His breathing a steady rhythm being done for him. I recently learned, thanks to an episode of Grey's Anatomy that 95 percent of patients who code, die. This statistic is not accurate, I also learned, but it prompted me to look it up. Studies that I located found that 35 percent of patients in ICU that code are resuscitated but only 12 percent ever leave the hospital. The odds seemed against Scott.

As the morning progressed, The doctors and nurses said they were pleased with his oxygen. The life support was breathing for him, but only partially. He was breathing partly on his own, meaning, he was a good candidate for coming off. To keep him on life support, he was sedated, but the sedation was "easy in, easy out," it was explained to me. As soon as they stopped the IV drip, he began to open his eyes.

He was unable to communicate, having the intubation tube in his lungs, but his eyes were opening. I still had no idea how long he had been without oxygen, and having watched doctor shows throughout my life, I knew that time frame was crucial to whether or not any damage had occurred to his brain.

The doctor's talked to Scott as though he was awake, only louder.

"Hey, Scott." We're going to see how well you can breathe on your own. If you understand, blink twice.

He blinked. Twice.

"Good job, Scott. This might hurt a little bit. Just hang in there, okay."

They then, slowly, began to reduce the oxygen that was being fed to him, allowing him to breathe on his own.. It was awful, and looked painful. At one point, I saw a tear fall from Scott's eye. I wiped it away, wondering what it meant. Was it a tear of pain, a tear of regret, a tear of fear?

They re-sedated him a couple of times and then determined that he was capable of breathing on his own. They painstakingly removed the breathing tube. He felt every bit of it giving us the first glimpse we would have at the damage that may have been done.

Once the tube was out permanently, he was able to communicate. His voice was strained, but it was clear that he was all there. It was glorious to know that despite the trauma he had been through, he was still Scott Schuler.

Chapter 8

Scott was delivering electrical supplies for Platt Electric in Albany, and listening to a lot of radio between 1992 and 1993. He had graduated high school, and attended what is later listed as "some college" on every form he's filled out forever. He got a great job as a delivery driver, but was destined for more. One day, he walked into KRKT off the street and asked to speak with the program director. Bill O'Brien, the award-winning morning show host and operations manager greeted Scott.

He explained to Scott that in order to "get into radio broadcasting," one should essentially be available at all times to board op, and also attend the station's events.

Scott listened and obeyed. He began going to the station's events, and ran the board for broadcasters on events. Board-opping doesn't mean air time, but he learned the ropes.

He would be given the evening slot, move up to middays (this is when I met him) then afternoon drive, and the two of us would take on the morning show together

He is the quintessential "life of the party. In fact, the party doesn't even begin until Scott arrives. This may be what attracted me to him. He was confident, far more than me. At 6 foot 6, and 350 pounds, he couldn't be ignored.

After my training with Scott, we really didn't cross paths for 2 more years. I worked overnight weekends for 3 months until I was promoted to the evening shift, 6 to midnight. Scott was on middays from 9 to 2, so we just didn't cross paths.

2 years after I started at the radio station, our company upgraded our broadcast software. A training was held so I had to go into work early to learn how it operates. The entire team of broadcasters was there, including Scott.

We did the training in one of the production rooms. There was some flirting, I recall. He was actually flirting with me! That day, or another, we decided to make a golf date. Innocent enough, we both had significant others at the time, but it was just golf.

We began golfing as often as time allowed. It was here that our opposing radio shifts came in handy. He didn't work until 10 am, so we hit the links before his shift. I was able to go home and rest before my 6 pm shift. Still just golf.

A turning point came at a funeral of all things. Our co-worker had been tragically killed, and our boss gave the entire staff the day of his funeral off. We all attended of course, and I sat with Scott. My emotions were high thinking of my co-worker's family, and of course this upset me to tears. Scott comforted me. After the funeral, with no responsibilities for the day, we headed back to Scott's house. We spent the afternoon in his living room just chatting and really getting to know each other. I was really starting to like him.

Our relationship progressed after that, but we kept it friends only as I still had a boyfriend, and he, a girlfriend. At this point, though we knew time was ticking on both of those relationships. In late July of 1999, we took our relationship to a romantic level, and never looked back. We were married in 2004, had our first child in 2006, and then 4 more children between 2010, and 2017. In 2018, we relocated to Lebanon and built a house on a wooded 5 acre lot. This is where he woke up on December 6th, complaining of a rapid heart rate.

It was a Monday. Scott had been up and down all night. When I finally woke up, he told me he couldn't get his heart rate down.

"It's just anxiety." I reasoned.

I am always unsympathetic when he is sick, and he is always "dying" when he is sick.

He explained that he'd been trying techniques he knew and nothing seemed to work. At around 6 am, he went to work.

On Mondays during the school year, the kids and I attend a homeschool co-op. I was on my break from teaching classes when my husband called me from Lebanon E.R. actually, if I recall, it was a text.

12/6/21 9:34 am

Scott: Urgent cares did ekgs, I' in a fib driving to ER. i'm ok but need to get under conrol .

9:48 am

Scott: At ER

Me: Ok

Thank you

Do I need to come?

Scott: No, IV meds are first

Just getting started

10:15 am

They might do the shock thing too. They do it all the time.

Me: Oh jeez! Ok

Scott: 10:29 am

Trying.Meds first

10:43 am

I love you baby

10:50

Meds now

11:22

Getting ready for shock thingy. One more round of meds first.

11:37

No covid

11:46 am

Putting me under in a few. Love you and the kids

I had been teaching my classes, and not checking my texts.

1:02 pm

Gonna need a ride here soon.

In and out, just like that. Crisis averted, or so we thought.

He took it easy for the next week. We tried to figure out what lead to this. Was it alcohol? Was he dehydrated? We both did research, and he made some changes.

His weight had gotten out of control and had been for several years. No begging, pleading, threatening, or promising on my part made any difference. This medical emergency seemed to make a difference.

He drank water, and only water, and started back on his Optavia weight loss meal plan. He had once lost 100 pounds with that program, but that had been 11 years ago.

I was excited for the changes he was making, hopeful that he could be a part of our family again. For so long, the kids and I ran circles around him as we went on adventure after adventure without him. He may have wanted to join us but for much of it he was physically unable.

Christmas was coming, and with 5 kids, we were busier than ever. There were presents to wrap, and there was magic to make.

One evening, I was wrapping presents in our bedroom, watching a Hallmark Christmas movie. A commercial for one of those medications came on. The medication had a million side effects. I glanced up and saw that it was medication for Atrial-fibulation. The narrator said:

"A-fib is one of the leading causes of stroke."

Unable to hold back, I threw down my tape and wrapping paper, and stormed out into the living room.

"You're going to have a stroke, and you're going to survive! We're going to bring you home an invalid, and you'll have a bed in that front room." The room we use for school, and toys, and guests. I imagined a hospital bed with my husband in it, unable to communicate normally, just existing, and no longer the man I married.

"Your kids will have to walk by your room every day and see their dad like that. Is that what you want?"

I was livid, convinced his poor choices had gotten us here. What other explanation could there be. He was over 400 pounds, and closer to 500, I was fairly certain. No mentally healthy person does that to themselves, and it had affected everyone around him for too long.

Of course he tried to reassure me that he was on a new path, and that none of what I was ranting about would happen. He'd been scared straight and was now on the straight and narrow. I had heard similar words before, however, and wasn't swayed from my doomsday prediction. I was trying to scare him straighter.

We went on with Christmas plans and general adulting/housekeeping duties.

On December 8th, Scott bought tickets for the Santiam Excursion Train. It was to be a Christmas surprise for the kids, and the tickets were for the December 18th ride. The train travels from Lebanon to Sweet Home. There and back it takes about 2 hours. Santa Claus rides the train, there are games, and treats, and that good old Christmas magic we try to manifest.

His heart rate fluctuated over the next week, and the following Tuesday, shortness of breath got the best of him. Again, he went to the E.R. This time, they located the blood clots.

This time, I was at work, and had no idea there was even an issue. Scott called me to explain the latest development.

"I'm at the E.R. again. They think my shortness of breath is from blood clots. They're doing some tests."

I don't know why, but I still wasn't overly concerned. Perhaps because of my limited medical knowledge, or my mostly positive outlook. I wrapped up at the office, and headed home to the kids, knowing they were on their own.

Our kids are 15, 11, 9, 6, and 4. The 11 year old, Sunny, is mature for her age, and generally in charge when they're home alone, which is very rare. But she and the 9 year old butt heads quite often. Leaving them on their own is a brand new phase we are in, and we max our time away to about 2 hours. Scott and I have arranged that someone is always home with them. It's how we are able to homeschool and work full time. I stay with them in the first half of the day, homeschooling, and working from home, while Scott goes to the office. He comes home early afternoon and I head to the office until the early evening.

When I get home from work, December 14th, a Tuesday, the kids were doing what they usually do. Some on tablets, others watching TV, my 15 year old in his room on x-box. It had been 8 days since their dad had his heart shocked back into proper rhythm, and now he was back in the E.R.

He called shortly thereafter to inform me that scans indeed show blood clots in his legs, and possibly in his lungs. Lebanon E.R. beds were full and their plan was to transport him to Corvallis for treatment. I recall being less concerned and more irritated with the inconvenience of all of this. Obviously I was naive to the severity of his condition.

"I'm just waiting for the ambulance."

"The ambulance!" I said. "There goes your shop."

I was under the impression that an ambulance ride bill was outrageous. We had recently refinanced our house with cash out to build a shop. I was now convinced that all of that cash we had taken out would be headed for medical bills.

He needed a few items from home, so I gathered them up. I threw his bi-pap machine, clean socks, underwear and a clean shirt into a bag and headed to the E.R.

When I arrived, I found him in the same room that our daughter had gotten 13 stitches in her leg three years ago on the 4th of July. She had slipped on loose gravel in our driveway and a jagged piece of rock ripped open her leg just below her knee. It was the most gruesome injury I had seen. I was amazed how well the E.R. doctor had been able to stitch her back together.

Scott took up the whole bed, and looked terribly uncomfortable. He smiled regardless. We chatted a bit about the plan for transport. He was scared.

"Hold my hand." he said.

"Why?" I asked, still irritated.

"Because it feels good."

So I did. I held his hand, not knowing what the coming days would bring, and certainly not anticipating what did come.

I visited him on Wednesday in Corvallis after he had been an admitted patient for a night. He was sitting in a chair with an i.v. drip of blood thinning medication.

Thursday night, our friend, Charlie visited him. Charlie is a nursing supervisor at the nearby Corvallis Clinic. He and Scott palled around in high school and remain close to this day. That night, Charlie texted me.

Charlie Wilson 12/16/21 8:20 pm

Honestly, Angie I'm worried about him...he didn't look good today...he was extremely short of breath with just sitting at the side of the bed...I'm sure he'll be fine but I hate seeing him like that.

I revealed Scott's downhill slide heath wise and my frustration with my inability to change it. This would be the beginning of unmasking our family's dirty little secrets. Honesty became my medicine, my therapy, and my treatment.

Charlie: That sucks! I sure hope he can make some lifestyle changes when he gets out of the hospital...I hope you and the kiddos are doing ok. And...if there's anything I can do to be a positive influence for him let me know and I'll do it.

Charlie's medical experience and close friendship with Scott had lead him to his concerns about Scott's appearance. I look back on this text and realize that Charlie knew how bad it was, and was trying to tip me off. He became a sounding board for me in the coming days and weeks, and I can't express how thankful I am for him and his family. They rescued all of us in many ways that will soon be unveiled.

Chapter 9

It's December 18th. My husband is 49 years old today. Everyone that comes into his ICU room wishes him a happy birthday. He is in no mood to hear it or to celebrate it. His heart has stopped, he was on life support for more than a day, and now his throat is raw from the life support tube being removed. He's also in extreme pain from the chest compressions that were performed on him to resuscitate him.

It is not lost on me that his life support was removed on his birthday. The irony, or serendipity of that causes me to look up often and shake my head in disbelief. You see, I had said a prayer not long before this medical journey all began. I had prayed that something would rock my husband, that God would shake him awake, to show him the changes he needs to make. This was not what I had in mind.

Scott was talking and from what anyone could tell, it seemed that being without oxygen for a time hadn't profoundly affected his capacities. I later learned from him that he didn't recall waking up that Tuesday morning short of breath, he didn't recall being admitted to the ICU, and he had no recollection of his heart stopping experience. Good, I thought. Who would want to remember that kind of trauma?

The staff in the I.C.U. was exceptional. They paid excellent attention to my husband, and met all of his needs. His butt hurt. That was the biggest problem in his mind. Unable to move as a result of being on life support for more than a day, he relied on nurses to rotate his body for comfort. Remember, he is a very large man. This process was not easy. It required several people and often the harness above. He required half a dozen pillows placed underneath him for relief. From side to side he went, and these were major events every time it was required. Unable to walk he would not be getting out of bed for some time. He was able to raise his left arm, but his right arm was useless at his side. His voice was rough and raspy from the irritation of the intubation. The baby steps of getting him moving were terribly frustrating.

Having been away from my kids for an entire day, I was thrilled when my sister and law and mother in law brought them to the RV. It was, after all, their dad's 49th birthday and his first re-birthday. I spent a few moments with them, loving on them and hearing about their adventures the previous day that I had missed. Our neighbor, Sarah had come to my house and orchestrated clean-up of our house, getting everyone involved. They may not have loved that, but I certainly did. She also provided dinner. My soldiers were organizing behind the scenes as we had no idea how long our stay at the hospital would be.

The kids devised a plan to do a birthday parade for their Dad. Julie took them to the Dollar Tree to get supplies. They busied themselves making giant poster board signs. Cowboy came to visit them and they roped him into the parade as well. On a cold, December 18th afternoon, my kids, their Aunt, and a local sheriff's deputy marched up and down Samaritan Drive. Scott's new room had a view of the road. I got great video of them, and my spirits were lifted by my wonderful, thoughtful children. They were finding joy in something awful.

As they day dragged on, I knew I would be spending the night again, however, I would not be sleeping in the RV. My big, strong husband was terrified, and asked me to stay in his room. I understood his fear, the last time he remembered going to sleep, he doesn't remember waking up.

I got a hospital issue blanket and pillow, and slept on the chair near the window behind Scott's bed. I use "slept" loosely, but even the couple of hours I did get revived me. Nurses were in and out all night checking vitals, rotating my husband's body, and getting him water. His mouth was terribly dry from the life support tube.

FB post

We are sitting up, we are eating soup, and even nearly was able to stand for a moment with assistance. He's already met all of the goals for today. I'm told his recovery this fast is beyond their expectations. Everything wears him out. Physical therapist came today to whip him into shape and she's tough. I think I want to be her when I grow up. Scott is an agreeable, but surly patient, cracking jokes like normal. He is in quite a bit of pain in his chest and arms. He's asking about the homefront being handled. I've been blessed to not have to concern myself this weekend as my mother in law, sister in law, nieces and many other family friends are on top of it. I now know that I much prefer being on the giving/ providing for others side, but I'm certain that I have grown and will continue to grow experiencing this side of it. As I told my friend in a text, I love being a part of this cycle of giving and can't wait until it's no longer my turn. I hope that doesn't sound ungrateful. I'll spend many days trying to find the words to say thank you. I hope to be able to get home to the kids soon, but Scott's having a hard time letting me leave, which I understand. He was even a bit fearful to go to sleep last night. The last time he willingly had, he doesn't remember anything else afterward (another blessing). That is the latest.

It dawned on me, in the night as I lie awake, my mind racing, that this was to be the day that my kids, their dad, and I were scheduled to ride the Santiam Excursion Christmas Train. Those tickets went to waste, as we missed our train.

I began to mourn the day I should have had and expressed it in my update that day. More brutal honesty, no more hiding.

December 19th, 2021

Usually this week I'm creating fantastic Christmas memories for the kids. The last week before we tear all the decorations down. We were going to make ugly sweater Christmas cookies Friday, go on the Christmas train Saturday (scott had bought tickets) and I was going to take each child shopping for a gift for their sibling whose name they drew. I was going to assemble scotts birthday gift, build him a drill and battery holder, finish the kids' teeter totter in time for Christmas, finish wrapping presents, and plan for the weekend but something else came up and I am now needed elsewhere and it's bumming me out a little. Could also be the weather.

Do I need anything? I don't actually know until I Need it if that makes sense. Sometimes I don't know what I need until someone takes it upon themselves to insist I need it and takes action without my permission. I actually prefer that and will strive to do that more for others. I've always been a person that anticipates needs and just takes action but I see how vital that is when everything around is chaos and unknown.

"Somebody somewhere wishes my worst problem was their worst problem." this is one I repeat to myself often, long before this. It keeps life in perspective. I still have that perspective and recognize all of my blessings. Some have expressed to me that they wish they could do more. I'm not sure how to convey that you have probably done the exact right thing without even knowing it. From the perfect words at the perfect time. A gift, a meal, checking in, a prayer, a call, a card, an offer, a thought, a visit, or a visit attempt that didn't work out. When I get downtime, and I remember each individual blessing, I hope I've been able to tell you that it was not only important to me but also that it came at the right moment.if I haven't yet, you'll be hearing from me.

I don't know what I'm doing. So I just keep doing it. I'm here in this experience that I knew would come and did everything I could think of to try to prevent. All those years of worry and frustration and it happened anyway. And he survived and I want him to continue making strides that feel tiny but are truly leaps. But I'm also transitioning to praying for his soul and mind to be healed. For him to treat himself with respect and love. For him to truly experience life with our kids and not just exist as it happens around him. It's out of my hands. I know that and I've always known that but it didn't stop me from trying. So I'm trying to figure out what to do next.

Wow! That's a lot for me to share. Welcome to what's in my head

The responses lifted me up, and my message prompted some to take immediate action, which I was not expecting. I truly had no expectations with my message, I just needed to vent my thoughts. Kind of like I'm doing now, with no expectations other than to share the stories of the experience, and the kindness that was shown to my family.

My social media posts were making the rounds, and Scott's situation was now known in our community. I received a message from the owner of the local car dealership, South Pacific Auto Sales. Another client of Scott's, they had also become friends. That's small town radio.

Brady Sell: Hi Angie, I'm not sure what's going on with Scott but I'd like to put something up on our digital reader board is that ok with you. Either way your family is in our thoughts and prayers. I hope all is well.

My friend, Kayleen devised a day with Lincoln. She and our first born had always had a bond. She picked him up the following day and took him to the new Spiderman movie. They chatted about the situation. Lincoln is honest and expresses himself very well. He doesn't hide behind anything, and I'm thankful that Kayleen was a sounding board for him.

Kayleen is 5 foot 1. We have a photo of her with Lincoln from a Christmas party many years ago. Lincoln was, maybe 7, and shorter than Kayleen. He now stands 6 foot 4. We decided it would be fun to recreate that photo.

When the two of them were out, they drove by South Pacific Auto Sales and Lincoln was able to see the reader board sign tribute to his Dad.

I handed my keys over to our neighbors, Ken and Sherri. They drove the kids to the store to go shopping for gifts. Normally I am in control of my household, but it was all out of my hands now as I spent day and night at the hospital this week before Christmas. They took my car, because it was the only way to transport 5 kids and 2 adults. They spent the day shopping, and the kids enjoyed it so much. I imagine Ken and Sherri enjoyed it as well. Afterward, everyone went to the Hall house to wrap up their gifts. Their house is about 200 feet away from ours so we bounce back and forth often. The thoughtfulness of this broadsided me. Everyone, busy with their own Christmas activity was squeezing time for my kids. It knocked me off my feet.

Angie contacted me (most people were calling/texting daily, some hourly). She announced that Alva had something for me, and could I come downstairs. Alva works in maintenance and IT at the hospital. Apparently it had been a slow week, so he occupied himself building the drill/battery holder I had mentioned in my post. It was far better craftsmanship than I would have done. I met him in his truck downstairs, and we drove to my vehicle in the lot to transfer it over. It was so heavy and wonderful. Again, his generosity took my breath away. How was I ever going to express my gratitude to the collective and individuals? This book. That's how. I was so excited to have the new addition to our garage under the tree for Scott in case he made it home for Christmas.

My sweet friend, Heidi had started a go-fund-me account in anticipation of astronomical medical bills. I saw the amount increasing each day, but I hadn't been brave enough to look at who was donating. It broke my heart to know that people I know and love, and some I didn't even know yet were going to work every day to make money to pay for their wants and needs, but still putting some aside for my family.

I received a call a day or two after my husband became responsive again. Chris Fairchild, my sheriff's deputy angel that had been so pivotal in my strength early on in this journey, told me he had an envelope for me. I had already decided to check in at work on my way home for a quick visit, so we agreed to meet in the radio station parking lot. His patrol vehicle was parked when I arrived. He explained that some people don't like donating online, but wanted to help and had written checks, or given cash. One, was his sweet mother, Karen, and his Dad, John.

Karen had worked at the golf course where Scott and I began our friendship. We had golfed a lot in those days, as I shared earlier, so we got to know her, and Fern, and the other ladies that worked the clubhouse quite well. Karen is as kind as a person can be so it's no wonder she raised a wonderful son like Chris, Cowboy, Fairchild.

Another check was from a high school friend of Scott's who owns his own electric company. Our paths have crossed with Kyle Patrick many times over the years, personally and professionally. I stood in the parking lot holding the envelope, stunned at the generosity. Breathtaking is the best way to describe being on this side of giving. I much prefer the other side, but the lessons I learned are priceless, and the growth I experienced from welcoming help is significant.

The meal train that my sister-in-law had set up was also in motion, and my family was well taken care of while I was gone. Our refrigerators and freezers were full. Some dropped the food off on the porch in a cooler, others stayed to visit with the kids. Still others brought gifts and activities.

My kids returned home one afternoon to a basketful of gifts for them on the porch. A lot of thought had been put into the gifts, and there was something for everyone. They had no idea who left it. We later learned it was from our other neighbors, the Medford family.

One of my favorite texts came from my friend, Karen Kutsch.

Karyn Kutsch, 12/29/21 7:40 pm

Hi Angie...this is Karyn...Shawn and I want you to know we are here for you too. We are going to Costco Friday morning and will be getting you some things you need...want. Shawn told me to tell you that "no" wasn't an option so we can either bring stuff you guys may like or if you please give us a list we can get stuff we know you guys want...need. Like food...laundry soap...whatever...we care about you and Scott and your family so much. You are just a kind and caring family.

So "no" wasn't an option. This made me smile so much, knowing Shawn. Another friend of Scott's from high school, they had been in our lives for many years. We also made the connection with Karyn as she is my friend, Angie's sister. Shawn had been experiencing some medical issues of his own at this same time, so here we are again. My faith in humanity has never wavered, not once knowing that people like Shawn and Karyn walk this earth.

Chapter 10

I have found myself in awe of the acquaintances, and even strangers that came to my aid throughout my husband's hospitalization. I had to keep reminding myself that my close friends and family also deserved recognition for the support they demonstrated. It's easy to overlook their contributions because we already enjoy a village mentality. We all step up when necessary without a second thought, and without thought of return.

My neighbor's son was supposed to come over Friday morning. In the morning I raced to the hospital to find out if my husband would live another day. I texted Sarah that I couldn't watch Grady, and explained what had gone down.

Sarah is a doer, and she quickly got to work rearranging her day. It's Christmas break, and Grady didn't have school. She is an electrician, which is certainly not a work-from-home job. Like many women, Sarah is expected to parent like she doesn't work and work like she doesn't have children, so I had watched Grady a few times so she could punch out her day.

Once she knew what my day was going to be like, she rearranged everything and came straight to my house. She provided dinner for my children and got them involved in household chores. I don't know a lot of details about those early days at home. I was staying at the hospital, so what was going on at home was out of my hands and out of my control. Sarah wanted my focus entirely on Scott.

She and I are eerily similar creatures, and we laugh that we both bought the property and built houses within 100 yards of each other. We are both physically strong females, we were both raised with difficult mothers who are still living, but no longer a part of our lives. We both love our children and love the challenges of raising them. Sarah and I both try to be the best versions of ourselves, but somehow we don't compete. I admire her strengths, rather than envy them. When she is capable of a task that I am not, I simply thank her and recognize how skilled she truly is. This probably makes her uncomfortable, but I don't care. She's exceptional.

We did chat by phone as she took over the functions of my house as well as continuing with her own. Her husband is a firefighter/paramedic and often work multiple shifts over several days. She didn't bother me with any of the goings-on at my house, but only wanted updates on Scott to relay to those who asked her.

Just before Christmas, I was home, and Sarah had made a quilt for me. Another of her many talents, I had heard her plans for quilts for important people in her life, including her child's teacher. I saw the inspired planning and care that she took with her projects. They were a reflection of her appreciation and love. I never once thought she put the same planning and care into a quilt for me. The gift took my breath away. Although it's a Christmas quilt, it will stay on my couch year-round.

I don't know how many meals Sarah made for my children, or how many loads of my laundry she folded. She likely doesn't know either and has never once brought it up since. Friends that come to your aid and then never bring it up again are a true gift.

In many cases throughout my husband's hospitalization, the smallest gestures came through at exactly the right time. After a few of these, I finally stopped marveling at each divinely timed occurrence and just let them happen, while looking up and smiling, feeling invisible arms around me.

12 hours after the phone call that changed our Christmas, I received this message:

Angela, we are thinking about you all and praying. I can't even imagine. You probably don't know this, but I work in a cardiac/interventional cath lab at Salem Hospital and we do procedures to treat clots specifically. I'm wondering where his clots are? And if he had a procedure for these clot busters or other? -September

No, I didn't know that she worked in a cardiac/interventional cath lab at Salem hospital. How did I not know this? Because I'm a jerk, and never once asked September, "So what do you do?"

September is a friend of friends and our paths have crossed a handful of times. I watched a college football game at her house that she shares with her husband, Dustin, and their adorable daughters. Dustin and Scott went to high school together (a familiar theme). Many of my friends are married to men who went to high school with my husband.

My interactions with September were always pleasant, but I kept her at arm's length. I'm not sure why. Perhaps I felt intimidated by her and put up a protective wall when I was around her. She was always kind regardless of my unfounded anxieties about her.

A source of vital information over the next few weeks, I was now texting her and calling her without hesitation. As they after a few cocktails, my inhibitions disappeared.

Chapter 11

Christmas was a week away.

The next day, he was moved to a neighboring ICU room. This room seemed to be for patients who are recovering. There were less machines, and buttons, and a larger harness was accessible here. The room was also larger. There was a chair near the window that would be my bed for the night. The nurses and doctors were telling Scott that he was going to be their "success story." Evidentially, leaving ICU alive isn't the majority of patients. The staff were determined to make a "success story" out of my husband.

As I prepared to head to the RV for sleep, Scott asked me not to leave. I suspect, terrified to go to sleep, as the last time he recalled having gone to sleep, he didn't recall waking. The nurses loaded me up with pillows and a blanket or two. I slept near the window, which grew colder with every hour. The uncomfortable chair folded into a pseudo bed. I lined it with pillows to lie on top of to take away some of the stiffness. It didn't work, but I was exhausted and slept for a couple of hours. His birthday was over, tomorrow would just be another day closer to Christmas.

His first visitor would be his best friend Alex. A cousin explained to me that as a child, Scott always introduced Alex, not as "Alex," but as "my best friend, Alex." As in, "My best friend Alex is coming over." "My best friend, Alex and I have a math test tomorrow." You get the idea.

Alex was the best man in our wedding. Former military, Alex lives on the East Coast. He has had a successful post military career, he's married to a fantastic lady, and has 2 beautiful children. He and Scott have stayed close, but like any long distance friendship, the check ins and visits were sparse. Alex and his wife, Whitney had visited 2 Christmases prior and it was pure joy.

Upon learning of his friend's condition, Alex bought a plane ticket immediately. He would have arrived in town the following day, however, in his haste and emotional state, he purchased the wrong ticket, and didn't fly out until the following day. I can't imagine his dread not knowing how he would find his friend, a day later than planned. I felt the same dread for him.

Alex came to the hospital on Saturday. He came straight up to the ICU. I had approved him as the day's visitor, he checked in, and was allowed in.

He was asked by staff if he had recently had any symptoms of Covid 19. He explained to them that he had not, but that he just stepped off of a plane. This fact caused enough fear in him that he opted to get a rapid test, which ironically, was not offered at the hospital. He would have to find a testing site, on a Saturday, and then wait for the results before he could come back. He would not be back this day.

My husband seemed to be on the slow mend. The TPA clot buster medication had by all evidence, blown out the blood clot that caused his pulmonary embolism. The focus, now, became preventing further clots, and getting his faculties back. One day on life support, I was told takes at least a week to recover from. Scott was unable to take care of himself, and with fluids being pumped into him, he was heavier than ever before.

The nurses spent the week working on getting his mobility back. I knew that being sedentary was not ideal for his condition. Blood clots often form when a person is immobile for a long period of time. Scott was still unable to get out of bed. ICU staff moved his legs for him.

Another night in the hospital with my husband, sleeping in a chair, I began to see that I wouldn't be vacationing in the luxury RV much. I did rely on it for meeting visitors who weren't allowed up, and for a quick change of clothes, or a bite to eat, but I spent most of my days that week before Christmas in Scott's room.

By midweek, I had convinced my husband that I needed to go home at night. I was desperately missing my children. They had been without me far more than any of us enjoyed.

My kids are homeschooled. We are together all day, every day, except for the few hours I slip away to work in the afternoons. I pull my strength from them. Maybe it's codependence, I'm not sure. I often joke that I spent my life looking for "my people," but never found them, so I made my own.

That first night home with my kids since the previous Thursday was bittersweet. I felt terrible leaving their dad alone, but knew, for my own mental and physical health, I needed to be with them. I arrived home late, perhaps at 9 pm. It was a good thing I prepared myself for a house in disarray.

The kids were all sitting on the couch, watching a movie. In the kitchen was an overturned container of cheese powder. The lid was off and some was spilled on the floor. It was obvious a little hand had been repeatedly digging in for a scoop. My 12-year-old daughter, Sunny had made popcorn, and the cheese powder was delicious sprinkled on top. Left low enough to reach, the jar will be consumed on its own.

I decided to care about the mess later, and also to clean it up later. We all chatted and hugged, and I explained my day to the kids. It was a glorious, messy, cheese powdery homecoming that I'll always remember.

That night, I was able to tuck my kids into bed like I do every night. They hadn't seen their Dad in two weeks. I kept the details of his condition superficial. They hadn't talked to him on the phone either. He wasn't quite up for taking or making phone calls. That would soon come though.

Scott and I had built our daughter, Sunny a loft bed the previous year. She had a full bed underneath for her sleepover guests but decided it took up too much room. While their Dad was hospitalized, I moved the full sized bed into the master bedroom. Having always dreamed of a wall-to-wall family bed, I slid the full size bed right next to our king, and achieved my dream. Now I could have all my kids sleep in my room with me. That night, everyone but the oldest snuggled together in our new bed. Lincoln decided to just lay with us for a while before retiring to his privacy.

I woke early the following morning after just a few hours of sleep. I got the house in order, laundry finished, dishes washed and put away, and directions for the kids scrawled out on a note. I wanted them to have some direction and responsibility, hoping it would keep them out of getting into too much trouble. Their Aunt and cousins would once again be stopping in to keep watch, but not the entire day. Parts of the day, they would be on their own.

This became my new routine. Waking early, around 5 am or whenever sleep decided to end. Putting the house in order, and assigning tasks for the kids while they slept. They would awake to a parentless house and a note. I wouldn't return home until 9 or 10 at night to grasp my sweet babies, stroking their backs in our giant bed until they fell asleep.

Before leaving after my first morning home, I decided the pile of burnables in my garage and pantry needed to be dealt with. I carted everything out to the fire pit. The morning was chili but not unbearable. As I was lighting the cardboard on fire, a pickup pulled into my driveway.

I didn't recognize the truck as a regular at our house. The driver parked, retrieved something, and got out.

"Angie! I'm here to clean your house."

Toting his caddy full of cleaning supplies, Josh "Sprout" Morris had carved out his morning to clean my house.

"I was here the other day, and it looked, well, sort of cluttery," He announced.

Trying not to take it personally, I thought to myself, "What do you expect? It's Christmas!"

So I smiled, appreciative of him not asking what he could do to help and instead telling me he's here to help. He had come by a day or two prior to check on my kids, who didn't know who he was. Sprout is another softball acquired friend of my husband. Spout is one of the masterminds behind all of his softball buddy's nicknames. My husband is "Schoolboy."

The cardboard burned fast, and I was ready to head to the hospital when Sprout handed me a Christmas card. I opened it and found an extremely generous amount of money. If you had asked me 10 days before who I thought would show up to clean my house, check on my kids, and help pay medical bills to come, I probably couldn't have guessed it would be Sprout!

After a hug and a heartfelt "Thank you," Sprout had one more request.

"Hey, uh, don't tell anyone about this. I like to do this on the down low," he said.

So I didn't tell anyone, until now. Sorry Sprout, but I can't leave this one out.

With it appearing that Scott on the other side of near disaster, my sister in law was returning to work and unable to come by as early or as often. One day, late in the week before Christmas, I was extremely concerned for my kids being on their own all day.

The previous evening after I had arrived home from the hospital, my 4 year old daughter had been eating apple slices at the table. She grew quiet. I turned around from the living room couch and immediately realized she was choking. I flipped her upside down, and started forceful blows to her back. It didn't seem to be working at first. After what seemed like an eternity, the piece of apple seemed to dislodge. This event had happened just minutes after I had arrived home from my day at the hospital. What if it had happened before I got home, or during the day! Would my older kids have known what to do? I couldn't believe I was leaving them all day with such responsibility.

They were stepping up and showing such maturity, but I knew I needed more help.

Before I left the following morning, I send a group text to all of my neighbors, even the ones I didn't yet know very well. Most are within walking distance in our newly developed neighborhood. I asked that if they had a few moments to please pop in throughout the day to check on the kids. I explained my schedule and added a bit of humor. I explained that I just want to make sure they're eating more than just cheese powder.

Sarah had been at my house quite often in between her own home, and work. She was organizing meals in the evenings as they came to our house. Judy took the kids up to her house to do crafts. Brennan Moore, one of our newest neighbors brought her 3 girls down to play with our kids and get their mind off of reality for a bit. It was lovely how our pleasant little neighborhood came together for my family. This became somewhat routine, for neighbors to just stop by to check on the kids.

Back at the hospital, Scott was beginning new physical therapy, and he hated it. Everything was a struggle, and he fought the suggestion of doing anything physical. Some nurses were accommodating to his wishes, but others kicked him in the butt, knowing what was waiting for him at home. We all hoped that he would be physically able to go home for Christmas, which was now just days away.

One of Scott's difficulties was simply sitting up in a chair. As I mentioned, the fluids they'd been pumping into him had caused his weight to balloon. Different chairs of different sizes were brought in and nothing seemed comfortable to him. I explained, that at his size, nothing would be comfortable. The tough love had begun. I had held his hand and sobbed as he lay on life support, now that we were here, I was mad!

Two things can be true at the same time. Yes, I was extremely angry at him for neglecting his health to such an extent. I was impatient with the slow progress and his seeming lack of desire to speed it up, but

I also had compassion for my husband. I knew he wouldn't respond well to my anger, but it was difficult not to scold him. Less than a week ago, he had died. I had to consider the trauma he endured and wasn't addressing. He wasn't talking. Getting any response from him was like pulling teeth. Conversations were either small talk, or just me talking and getting one or two word responses from him. I was beyond frustrated and was beginning to snap at my husband.

I reached out to my friend, Jill that week. She had crafted personalized Christmas stockings for my kids and even one for our dog, Blue. She loaded them up with goodies, and delivered them to my house. She also, thoughtfully made Scott a funny stocking with antlers as well as ornaments to hang in his room.

Jill is extremely talented and crafty and runs a side hustle creating gifts. She explained that she had ordered extra stockings and had no use for them. She asked if I had a use for them. This generous offer gave me a great idea. With it looking more and more like Scott would not be home for Christmas, I knew the stockings would come in handy.

Christmas is Scott's favorite. He enjoys giving gifts to our kids, to me, to friends and family, and even to strangers. He loves having things stashed to give as last minute gifts to anyone and everyone. He even proposed to me on Christmas in 2003. Encouraging my new woodworking hobby, I had unwrapped a new radial arm saw that was under our tree. Thinking this was my "big gift" for the year, he gestured toward our hutch in our Brownsville, Oregon home that he and I had built together. On the glass shelf sat a tiny box, a ring box. I opened it and found a lovely engagement ring. At that point, we had been together for 4 years, and despite living together and owning a home together, we hadn't really even talked about getting married. I was stunned and he simply said, "So do you wanna?" We were married the following summer.

I suspected the thought of being in the hospital over Christmas was weighing on him. Maybe not. It's hard to tell day from night, let alone, Christmas day from any other day from inside the hospital walls. I made an executive decision anyway to bring as much Christmas to him as I could.

With Jill's help, I decorated his room. I strung lights, and hung his stocking. He had even received a tiny Christmas tree as a "get well soon" gift that we were able to decorate and display. My sweet friends, Angie and Alva struck again. Their daughter, McKenzie took the time to make Christmas decorations for Scott's room. I hung up her "Merry Christmas" banner and all of the Christmas cards he was receiving from KRKT listeners, friends, and family.

Hospital staff took noticed and seemed genuinely appreciative for the decorations. I was careful not to impede their work with any of the décor. I suspect I broke a few hospital rules in the process, but those were either ignored or overlooked by the kind staff.

I stayed throughout the day Christmas Eve, but left an hour or two earlier than usual. Before leaving, I told my husband that I would be back on Christmas after the kids had opened their gifts. Our sweet friend, Roger Nyquist owns the local bowling alley. He invited my family on Christmas day to come enjoy the facility. I was so thankful for such a wonderful offer for my family to look forward to. Their Aunt would meet them there, and I would be able to spend Christmas with my husband.

Christmas Eve broke my heart, but I was thankful to be home with plans of loading our tree up with gifts for our kids who have now been through so much. It's been nearly 3 weeks since they've seen their Dad. He had purchased gifts for them, and thankfully, prior to his hospitalization, had wrapped many of them. He had even wrapped gifts for me, and stashed them in his hiding places in our garage. I picked up the slack, and wrapped what he hadn't. I had been looking at those gifts all week, thinking to myself, "These could have been the last Christmas gifts Scott every bought for us." I was confident but cautious in my feeling that he would be coming home soon

I have always wanted to attend a Christmas even church service. Ordinarily our Christmas Eve is spent with family so it was not a possibility. There would be no Schuler family Christmas Eve gathering this year, however so I reached out to my neighbor, Sarah. I learned that the church she attended would be holding a service on Christmas Eve and asked if she's like to go. She agreed. We got our kids ready and rode together to Valley Life Church in Lebanon, OR. Even my reluctant teenager told me later that he was glad I made him go. The kids lit candles, sang songs, and had treats. They enjoyed a Christmas story and we thanked God for our blessings. Other friends of mine attended that evening, and made sure to inquire about Scott. I shed many tears at the warmth of their hugs.

Christmas morning with 5 kids is chaos, I try to maintain some order so everyone can savor the morning, but, there's so many gifts! Everything multiplied by 5, plus gifts from Aunts, Uncles, Grandparents, friends and neighbors. The kids were so excited for me to open a gift they had purchased when Ken and Sherri had taken them shopping. I tore off the paper to find a lovely new comforter for my bed. It was blue and grey striped and I made a huge fuss about how much I loved it. My 10 year old got a hover board and spent the morning trying to master that. By the late morning he was doing circles around the kitchen island. Everyone was thrilled with their gifts, and with the opportunity to face time their Dad.

We got Scott on the phone once the chaos had died down a bit. I wasn't sure how seeing his kids on Christmas morning over the phone would make him feel. I was hopeful, though that this would be the only time that would happened, and we would have many Christmases to come together as a family.

Scott seemed tired on the phone. His nurses had told me he'd been having trouble sleeping most nights. Plus, there are scans scheduled in the early mornings at times, and general hospital noise that interferes with any hope of a pleasant night's sleep.

"I want you to open your presents," he told me.

I resisted, not wanting to open anything from him until he was home, but he insisted. He told me where each one that he had wrapped was in the garage. I had to get out a ladder to get a couple of them. I opened a beautiful new pair of boots, a Cricut, and some of my favorite beverages, including some irish cream. He and I liked to put a splash in our Christmas morning coffee that I was drinking without him today.

He spoke with all of the kids, who were excited to show him all that Santa had brought to them. They were also quick to leave the conversation and get back to playing though.

We tidied up as much as one can on Christmas morning, got dressed, and headed for the bowling alley. Roger opened the doors early for our family. There's also an arcade, so I knew that I would have plenty of time to visit with Scott while the kids had a blast with their Aunt and cousins. Roger covered all the cost for them and I thank him every time I see him.

Chapter 12

On my way to the hospital, I made a stop for fuel and wrestled with my morning plans. I wanted Scott to be able to give gifts at the hospital. I had gathered supplies for him to stuff the stockings that Jill had purchased too many of and gave to me. His favorite thing to give, though was lottery tickets. My dad had won $200 dollars on a Christmas scratch off we sent him one year. I knew I wanted to get enough lottery tickets for him to stuff the stockings, but I struggled with the thought of handing over that much money. I brushed the hesitation away knowing it wasn't for me, it was a gift for my husband.

I stopped at the Chevron in Tangent, OR. The Christmas day crew was an all-female crew. After asking for a fill, I headed inside. 3 women worked behind the counter, and two others were at the deli. Working on Christmas day. I wondered if that had been a tough decision, if they were getting overtime holiday pay, and if they had kids at home.

I purchased more than $200 in scratch off tickets. Some $1, some $2, a few $5 and even a handful of $10 scratch off tickets. Then, I decided to start Scott's giving right there. I asked the lady that had been my cashier if she was allowed to accept a lottery ticket from me. She said she was. I gave her one of the $5 tickets. I handed the same tickets to the other 2 ladies behind the counter. Then I went to the deli and gave those two women $5 scratch offs. Finally, when going back out to my car, I handed the gal who pumped my gas a $5 scratch off. I was looking forward to telling my husband. He would have enjoyed doing what I had done on his behalf.

Scott was awake and waiting for me to get there. Although I had been harsh in the preceding days, he looked forward to my visits. It broke up his long days in the hospital, I think. I explained that he was going to stuff stockings and distribute them to everyone that entered his room. I laid out a stocking stuffing station with all of the candy, gifts, and lottery tickets I had gathered. Scott was in his chair when I arrived (which he hated, remember?). He began putting candy slowly into a stocking, then tried tearing off a lottery ticket. These little tasks seemed to tire him out and he asked me to do it. I stood next to him stuffing all of the stockings until none remained empty and all were overflowing. Scott gifted them to his nurses, his physical therapists, his doctors, and the CNAs. They all expressed how grateful they were. On my way out later that day, I gave a stocking to the young man at admission that I had seen so much of in the previous two weeks. He was shocked and thankful as well.

Chapter 13

Snow was in the forecast, and a lot of it. A white day after Christmas was expected. Scott didn't want me to drive to the hospital in the snow, so we agreed that I wouldn't likely be coming in on December 26th, a Sunday. The snow began falling Christmas evening.

Our area of the Willamette Valley doesn't see a lot of snow. Some years, there's none. Other years, just a dusting. Once in a while we get a good dumping of snow, but usually it's just hope for snow. This was one of those good dumping of snow years. Several inches of snow fell overnight. The roads were virtually impassable and I was ready for a day of play with the kids on our property. I felt pretty comfortable taking a day off from the hospital, but guilty for leaving him alone at the same time.

First, I called my husband. He would generally answer my calls unless he was asleep, but would call me back once he woke up. I couldn't reach him, so I busied myself gathering up snow bibs, hats, gloves, and boots for the kids when they woke up. I tried Scott's phone several more times throughout the morning before going outside with the kids. We played until afternoon and wore ourselves out.

I spoke with my boss as well, and explained my plan to return to work the following day, Monday. We were discussing covering all of the shifts on air between, Glenn and me.

Pulling a sled, I headed toward my neighbor, Sarah's house. Her 6 year old son, Grady was outside throwing snowballs. Braddock, my 6 year old, and my 4 year old, Loxley stayed outside to play while I went in. I entered without knocking and found a toasty, roaring fire, Robbe and Sarah.

She gave me a beer, and we discussed the lack of progress in Scott's healing. Sarah offered wise words while her husband washed dishes. In times like these one never knows what will trigger emotion. Today, for me, it was Robbe washing the dishes. I started crying.

Scott had neglected himself so much, and taken on such bad habits, he was painfully absent. Unable to help, or even participate in our lives, he was drinking too much alcohol, and I felt like he was leaving the details of raising our kids and running our house to me. What brought the wave of emotion was that Sarah hadn't asked Robbe to wash dishes, he had simply noticed that they needed washed. I realized, that hadn't happened in our house, maybe ever, but certainly not in many, many years. I wanted that, a husband that was physically capable of getting up and washing dishes without being in pain and getting tired out. I wanted him to not be trapped in his own body anymore, to stop turning down invitations because he can't climb stairs, or they don't have a chair that can support him. The limitations are endless when a person is his size.

Sarah attended my pity party. She and two beers talked me through it. As I was gathering myself together, there was a knock on the door.

Judy Green, our neighbor up the hill had ridden her quad to Sarah's house. She had planned on asking Sarah how I was doing but was thrilled to find me there to ask herself.

Judy is a retired school teacher. She and her husband, Kerry built a lovely home with a bright red barn. Judy uses the upstairs as her crafting area. Prior to my husband's hospitalization, I had only interacted with them superficially via pleasant small talk.

"I just want you to know, I am available for whatever you may need, Angie" Judy began. "Day or night. I don't sleep well, so you can call me anytime for anything, okay?"

I would soon be calling on Judy.

Chapter 14

Still unable to reach Scott, I finally called the nurses station.

"Oh, hasn't anyone reached out to you?" the nurse asked when I inquired about my husband.

Scott had been readmitted to the Intensive Care Unit.

The nurse explained that he had extreme shortness of breath in the morning when he woke up. Scans showed clotting in his lungs again, and a potential for another pulmonary embolism.

40 minutes away down a snowy highway, I called my sister in law. She was just 15 minutes away from the hospital and agreed to go in as his caregiver that day. She gave me updates throughout the day as did the doctors and nurses who reached out by phone multiple times.

The clots were a real threat and there were a couple of options. One was to go directly to the clot and remove it. Another was to administer TPA, the clot busting drug that had already saved my husband once. It was explained to me that they didn't recommend the TPA because a second dose could result in a bleed, so they were hoping to do the direct to clot procedure and get him stabilized.

Another call from the on call doctor. He explained that because of my husband's size, they were unable to do the direct to clot procedure and that the only option would be to administer the TPA drug. He tried to reassure me that he believed my husband's youth was on his side and a bleed would not be likely. I had to give the okay, however, and I did. Then I waited.

I believe I must have told the kids what was going on, but I don't recall. They'd had such a beautiful day of play, and Christmas the day before. Now a new fear threatened their peace.

That evening, doctors administered TPA for a second time in just over a week to Scott. Scans showed that it broke up the clot, and now they would monitor him for bleeds. Julie stayed in his room as they asked him routine questions, checking his smile, his tongue, anything for a sign of a stroke. He passed the tests all day long.

Julie and I spoke throughout the evening.

Julie 4:34 pm

They just started the TPA infusion

They will check on him at 4:45 and every 30 min for 2 hours

Me: Cool. Just got off the phone with the doc

Julie: he just passed his 2nd neurological test. He's talking and being funny under his mask. He got a little anxious about 10 min ago. Wondering where he was exactly. He knows he is in the hospital but , I guess without his glasses he can't see very far. So he kept asking me what was above him.

It's snowing heavy again. I'm hunkering down for the night here.

Me: Okay, but Jack says he'll come get you if you change your mind.

Julie: Okay. I might but then I think no. Meh.

Julie 6:33 pm: More of the same. They are giving him a 2nd dose or what they call the other half. He get anxious when they take the bi-pap off so they put it back on.

He said he likes the music

Me (after speaking with doctor) Ok. So the half dose wasn't enough. Doc says he was going to try a lesser dose first then do the other half if it didn't work.

Julie: The doctor says they go by how Scott says his breathing is and feels. His oxygen is slightly better than it was but, they want to go ahead with the next dose.

Julie: I just heard the nurse tell the incoming nurse that there was "slight improvement but, due to patient response and size they are going ahead with 2nd dose.

Me: Roger. Nice eaves dropping.

Julie: Scott wants to know if you have any snow pictures from your house.

Me: I didn't take any

Julie 8:52 pm 2nd dose complete. Now more waiting and back on heparin now. They gave him trazadone for sleep and anxiety. They up'd his bi-pap pressure and turned the moisture part back on. Heart rate is 96.

Julie explained that she had asked the doctor what is going to stop the clot in his leg from going to his lungs again. The doctor had said that we just have to trust the body to do its thing.

I shared and update with everyone following this saga on social media.

December 26th

Any hope of having him home soon has been blown. (Edited to add: that is okay. I want him in the hands of the experts until this is taken care of and he can safely come home) After radio silence all morning from Scott Schuler I called the hospital to check on him. No making it in today obviously. The nurse said he had a rough morning, and was in sinus tachycardia, and they suspected a worsening clot. He does have a pretty severe pulmonary clot again, so they put him back in the i.c.u. They plan is for interventional radiologists to administer medicine directly to the clot to break it up. I'm told this is a better option than a general i.v. of the TPA clot buster medication which can result in bleeding. However, they said because he's young, it's a bit less risky, however still risky. I then asked, if it's common for a person who's had an i.v. drip of a blood thinner for 2 weeks to continue clotting. Doc said it's something they will explore the reason for once they take care of this emergency. Possibly he's resistant to the medicine, possibly it's a genetic issue, etc. Praying that this intervention takes care of the immediate problem, and that they can determine why he is continuing to clot and take necessary action. Everything seemed under control, and I went to bed late that Sunday night.

Chapter 15

My phone rang before midnight Monday morning. I had placed it on a charger on the bedside table, plugged into my computer tower. Turns out it hadn't changed at all and was at 4 percent. I shook off the sleep stupor and saw that my sister-in-law was calling. She had spent the night in i.c.u. with her brother.

"Hello?"

"Ang, Scott's having a stroke."

I could hear her voice shaking like she was on the verge of breaking down."

"Shit!" was all I could come up with, still not sure if I was awake or dreaming, but that had been the theme of the entire week.

"Okay," I said.

"You need to come, but you can't drive. It's too icy. Can you call Scott Bingham to bring you in."

My instinct to not bother anyone took over. I'm going to wake my friend Scott at midnight. I know he sleeps with a c pap machine and hated the thought of interrupting his slumber.

"I can make it. I've got 4 wheel drive. I'll just make it."

"No. it's really snowy here. It's snowing right now. The roads are probably terrible." she insisted.

After we disconnected, I dialed Scott Bingham. I had a text message from him that day so I just touched it and pressed the little phone icon. The call went to voicemail. Maybe, I thought, he's one of those wise people who turns his phone off at night when he goes to bed so that no one bothers him. Good for him.

Think! I can't. Who can I call that would be up at midnight? I hadn't shaken off the cobwebs yet. In addition to a ride, I also needed someone to come hang out in case the kids woke up. Judy. She had said, arriving at Sarah's carrying a bright orange helmet, "call me if you need anything."

I explained to her that I don't really know what I need until I need it, but I will reach out when I need help. I need help now. I dialed up Judy.

She answered quickly and sounded relatively awake for midnight.

"Judy? Scott is having a stroke at the hospital. I need to go. Can you come here so that if the kids wake up, you can tell them where I am?" I was surprisingly calm, but more than a week now of ups and downs had made me able to communicate coherently in a crisis.

"Yeah," she said. "I'll be right over."

"Okay. Thank you so much. I've got to figure out how I'm going to get there, but thank you."

I then heard her call to her husband.

"Kerry, Angie needs a ride to the hospital. Can you take her?" she asked. I heard his muffled voice in the background say 'sure,' along with background noise from a television.

"Kerry will take you, Angie."

"Okay. Wow. So I guess I'll just drive up and meet him." I'm still pretty groggy at this point.

"Well," she started, "he'll have to bring me down there, and then you guys can just leave from your house."

Judy and Kerry live at the very top of our neighborhood hill. So she would technically be driving "down" to my house. Their beautiful red barn is a neighborhood landmark. Judy does her crafting in the expansive upstairs while the downstairs serves as storage and a workshop for Kerry. The barn they built themselves and even lived in it temporarily while their home was being built.

She called back after we disconnected and reminded me that her husband may have had covid the previous week. They had driven to California with friends. Those friends had all tested positive. Kerry came down with a "cold" but couldn't find any at-home test kits. So he wasn't officially diagnosed but assumed he had covid."

"Do you still want him to take you?" she asked.

"Yes. It's fine. We can just both wear masks on the drive."

They arrived within 10 minutes but I knew we had to make tracks. The drive took 30 minutes when the roads weren't icy, and who knows what conditions we would encounter.

Kerry took the drive slowly; maybe 30 miles per hour. I felt incredibly safe in his big beautiful truck. We chatted on the way. Some about my husband, and some small talk. I welcomed the distraction. It beat thinking about the possible horrors awaiting me at the hospital.

We arrived just after 1 am. Kerry dropped me off at the Emergency entrance. I knew that at those hours, the main entrance wasn't open yet.

Emergency dept. personnel questioned me about whether or not they said I could come up to the I.C.U. We found out later that this is because my sister-in-law was already there, and it wasn't visiting hours. She, as the support person was allowed, but I, now just a visitor was not. The guy...maybe girl, I don't remember at the front desk called up to find out for sure. I was buzzed in, so I must have been given the okay. Rules are bent when your husband may be dying.

The next few moments are a blur, I just know I entered i.c.u. and found everyone in room 2004.

The first night I arrive, after being told his heart had stopped, he'd been in 2006. After they removed the vent he moved to 2005. Now we were in 2004. We had punched every room on that ICU south corner.

Somebody spoke to me, maybe Julie, maybe a nurse. As I said, it's a blur. I wrote this while journaling days later.

I headed straight for your room and found you, once again surrounded by medical professionals. Your sister was holding it together, processing the scene. Time to process the scene was not a luxury I was given. My memory of the moments after I arrived in your room is fragmented. I remember being apprised of the situation, much of it I knew. My legs started to feel weak, and the room began to spin. Completely unsure what was happening to me, I looked to the nearest nurse and quietly announced, "I think I need to sit down."

My sleep had been interrupted by that call from Julie. Asleep for maybe an hour, I had been charging my phone by the bed. A departure from my usual charging spot on the kitchen counter. Had it been there, I may have slept through the phone call.

Someone brought me a chair, and I sat down.

I'm in control. Always in control. This was new. My body was doing things I'd never experienced. Lack of sleep? Shock? Too much to process? All of the above? The right side of Scott's face was paralyzed. He was moaning, and his eyes were rolling around. His speech was incoherent. This was the beginning of my darkest hours.

I did some deep breathing, and got myself together enough to take in some information from the medical staff. Within a few minutes, maybe an hour, maybe longer, I was taken into a small room behind the main desk area to see the scans of my husband's brain. The neurologist, a confident, small, older man from California was in charge, and showing me the bleed. Another doctor, the on call doctor was in the small room with us.

"Is this something he can recover from?" I recall asking.

"Your husband is a very unhealthy man." The neurologist responded matter-of-factly with a touch of sympathy. I could tell he had delivered bad news before.

I took that as a 'no.'

I retreated, devastated, back to my husband's i.c.u. room. Back again, planning to spend the night in the stiff pull out chair bed by the cold window. Colder now that it had snowed. I looked out on the hospital campus. It was beautiful, like a Hallmark movie scene, but it didn't make a dent in my sadness. It was the middle of the night. I was alone with my moaning, incoherent husband and his endlessly beeping monitors. The I.C.U. was relatively quiet, and devastatingly lonely. I didn't sleep. Not at all. I sat, and let my mind lose control. I thought about my husband's line of work, speaking. He can't speak anymore. What now? He's only 49! I'll need a new line of work. We were so close to getting him home! What about the kids! Loxley's only 4! How will I raise them without him? Where will he live? Will we have to sell the house? The negative thoughts were out of control, and no matter how much I tried to reel them in, it was of no use.

Early in this journey, the thought that "Somebody, somewhere wishes my worst problem was their worst problem" could bring me out of any downward spiral. That phrase was completely useless. I was eyeballs deep in self-pity and fear. My brain was struggling, and failing to protect me.

My sister in law called me at the exact worst moment of my life

Meri is the woman who talked me through my first miscarriage. I called her on my drive home, sobbing. She had also experienced a devastating miscarriage and she told me what had helped her. She said all the right things. When I went no contact with my mom 7 years ago, she counseled me through the information I unravelled as I researched my emotionally neglectful childhood and toxic relationship with my mother. I swear, Meri is the reason I didn't have to pay for therapy. Thousands of miles away, she is my rock, always.

I sobbed, and unintelligibly attempted to convey all that I was feeling. She listened. She validated. She related. She said all the right things again. Then she handed me over to my brother.

This was tough for him.

Our relationship is different.

We fought, like siblings do, but we weren't encouraged to love each other. I was useful to him as a child and teen when I could catch or hit fly balls with him. When we were playing sports together, we got along. So, I honed my skills in order to be as useful to him as I could be. I always loved him, and wanted so badly to have a relationship with him. It was not allowed, however, in my house.

As a female in my home, I have since realized that I was competition for male attention. My mother needed all the male attention, and that included my Dad and my brother. It was unspoken, but known.

My brother enlisted in the Navy upon (barely) graduating high school. Within the year, free of my mother's influence, he had an epiphany. He apologized for his treatment of me, and I forgave him immediately.

From then on, our relationship improved. He's an exceptional human being, but he also struggles with the effects of our childhood, although he may not be as aware of it as I am. Although we are close, and love each other, it's difficult for us to say the words.

Isn't that funny? We can't say, "I love you."

We did in the early hours of December 27th.

Like his wife, he too listened to me unintelligibly sob my fear into the phone, probably getting soaked in tears, 1000 miles away in the process. My nose gets plugged up when I'm uncontrollably crying, so that made it even more difficult.

Not wanting my husband to hear my conversation, I had migrated to the "still closed for covid" waiting room that had become so familiar. Everything in this hospital had become familiar. The elevator, the staff, the cafeteria, the parking lot...

Despite the waiting room being "closed for covid," the fish were still being fed. At one point, I lay on the floor beneath the fish tank. The fish tank that was probably meant as a soothing element for those in fear, or grieving. I'm always in control! Why am I so out of control?

My brother did his best to love me over the phone. Despite my lack of control, I felt his compassion, and his worry for me. None of us have ever been through anything like this with me on this end of it.

In 2003, my brother was diagnosed with a rare cancer. Just before his diagnosis, he had been visiting Oregon. We were on the golf course, getting ready to play 9 holes. I offered him something, I can't remember what, and he informed me that he was becoming lactose intolerant and couldn't take whatever I was offering. Upon his return home to Rhode

Island (Where he was stationed at the time) He discovered a lump in his groin area. Thinking, "hernia," he made an appointment with his doctor, and non-Hodgkin's Burkett's Lymphoma was the diagnosis.

Our family took turns flying out to Rhode Island to assist. Mine may have been the 3rd or 4th shift after my mom, Meri's grandmother, and others. When I arrived, Jason was doing regular treatment for the cancer. He looked like a cancer patient. Gaunt, pale, and sick. I saw very little of my brother in the 2 weeks that I spent at his home in Rhode Island. He was spending much of his time in the hospital. I stayed back at base housing with Meri and my nephews, 3 year old Jace, and almost 2 year old Jaren. Jace would have his 4th birthday while I was there.

I cooked meals, I played with the boys, and I listened to Meri. We chatted, sometimes late into the night. Our unbreakable friendship was beginning to form.

For Jace's birthday, I remember, having bought a "How to make Balloon Animals" book at the commissary. I made balloon animals for his party.

When I flew home, my brother wasn't out of the woods. It was still touch and go. My mom would give me updates and they were dramatic and full of gloom.

I had gone for a run one day, and was struggling to finish without taking a break. I started making deals with God. After one particularly difficult mile, I said, "God! If I can make it home without stopping, my brother will survive this." Nothing stopped me after that.

Not only did he survive, he decided that running marathons was his new venture. He's run a dozen plus marathons and other race lengths. In 2014, we ran the Portland Marathon together.

I also spoke with my Dad, and didn't hold back anything. Very uncharacteristic of me, but under the circumstances, I didn't care.

I had spoken to my Dad on a daily basis.

I look just like my Dad, but as I get older, elements of my mom's physical beauty are revealed in me. That sure would have been nice in high school.

I dated a boy in high school. He was a junior and I was a senior. He was beautiful, and I wanted to marry him. I wanted to marry any boy that gave me positive attention in high school.

He broke up with me for a girl named Inga. I was devastated.

My Dad stood in my bedroom doorway, broken over my sadness, grasping for ways to help me.

"What do you want me to do?" He was at a complete loss, but desperate to help me heal.

I felt the same from him now. This had to be so hard for him. To see his 44 year old baby completely despondent and nothing he could do to make it better. While I felt so sorry for myself and my little family, I also sympathized with my tough, Vietnam Veteran Dad's struggle to ease my pain, which was impossible.

At close to 5 am, after being up all night, I had to reach out. I hoped someone would be awake. I cast out a text praying to catch an ear. Jill is the earliest riser. I texted her.

4:44 am, December 27 2021

"You are probably getting up soon. Scott suffered a stroke last night. He's in icu and they'll do a scan at 530 to assess. Whether it got worse or stayed the same. I'm at the hospital. I don't need anything. Just wanted you to know.

I only had to wait 10 minutes.

4:54 am

I love you so much...I love Scott so much...My heart is breaking for you going through this and of course Scott. Good Sam Regional and AGH have some of the best stroke teams; although, you never want it to happen, timing is everything in treatment and I am glad he was there. You are the strongest lady I know. I am going to start my unknown road condition trek in. Might take a bit loner but I can leave anytime to be with you, your kids, or run supplies. Thank you for letting me know. There are a couple local churches who have been praying for Scott. And I'll ask for more prayer power.

5:06 am

Thank you. Yes. More prayers. I'm having a hard time seeing a positive outcome from this.

This was the understatement of the year. I was drowning in sorrow.

With the morning light, I regrouped. Funny how night festers such hopelessness, and the sunrise can numb the hopelessness and bring energy to act.

At around 10 am, I sent a text to Jill expressing my frustration with the staff.

I recall feeling as though the doctors had given up on my husband.

Chapter 16

At this point, unable to be on blood thinners for a minimum of 2 weeks as a result of the brain bleed, doctors determined that Scott would need an IVC filter to control any clots passing into his lungs which could lead to another pulmonary embolism. The inferior vena cava is a large vein in the middle of your body. The device is put in during a short surgery. Veins are the blood vessels that bring oxygen-poor blood and waste products back to the heart.

I was vague in my text to Jill, out of respect for my husband's privacy. Samaritan informed me that they would not do the procedure. What I didn't tell Jill, or anyone else was the reason they wouldn't perform the procedure was because my husband was too heavy for the table that the procedure would be performed on.

Although the table could hold his weight, it couldn't hold his weight in the event that he coded again, because then, a medical professional would need to climb on top of him to perform life saving measures.

Julie and I pleaded with the on call Doctor to find a table at a hospital so that we can transfer him for the procedure. As though I had asked my child to "do the dishes" he shuffled away in a bit of a huff. A short time later, he revealed that he had made a call, to which hospital I don't know. Truthfully, I don't know if he made a call at all. He said, "If they don't have one, nobody does, but you're welcome to make some calls."

Is that how it is? These doctors who are paid exorbitant wages to save lives put the life-saving responsibility on family members? Having no experience in this environment I could only assume that this was either completely normal or complete bullshit!

Fortunately, we know people. Julie immediately called our cousin Joelle. Joelle works at Providence in Portland. Reaching back in my mind, I recalled September's offer to be there for any questions I may have. She picked up the phone when I called.

I explained the predicament we were in and inquired if the cath lab that she works for could A. support my husband's weight, and B. had availability for him immediately.

She hung up the phone with me, and immediately called her doctor

Joelle was also helpful and made the necessary calls to determine that indeed, their table could hold Scott.

We were on a mission to save my husband's life, but there was an underlying desire to put the doctor in his place too.

We made contact with OHSU in Portland. They too had a table that would support my husband's weight, and we were put on a waiting list to get him a bed to have him transferred. I could feel that everyone following this journey was in need of knowing what was happening. I shared...everything.

December 27th

Overnight complications. Not the news I wanted to share. Option a of a targeted attack on the clot turned into option b. He was administered the clot buster medication... for the second time in just over a week throughout his body. His pulmonary clot was wreaking havoc on his breathing so it was crucial immediate action be taken. it appeared to break up the clots. They then watched for signs of bleeding. He passed with flying colors...at first.

Julie Tatum noticed some concerning signs at about 11 pm. She called for the nurse and he was taken immediately for a ct scan. He suffered a small bleed in his brain and immediate action was taken to get it under control.

When I arrived at 1 am, he was showing the effects. 10 hours later, everything has improved immensely. A 6 am ct scan showed that the bleeds were unchanged. A dose of good news. He's awake, alert, talking, eating...doing all the right things.

The newest in a

long line of hurdles is that he now cannot be on the blood thinning medication for 2 weeks to prevent further bleeding. This is concerning because he still has clots and now they may grow. Let's all remember that his clots continued to grow even on the heparin drip. An ivc filter in his lung is the newest weapon to manage the clots in his lungs. He is being transferred to ohsu for the procedure.

A coordinated effort to manage the homestead quickly ensued. No sooner had I spoken allowed to the icu room my concern at leaving the kids, I had a message from Becky Bathke asking if she could go to my house. Neighbors are spending the day and night today. I warned the kids they will be seeing lots of faces in the coming day/days... just maybe not mine.

A middle of the night phone call sent my neighbors, judy and kerry to my house. One to wait for the kids to wake up, the other to drive me in. When I called to check in on them, I heard Sarah Boren's voice. It's like tag team childcare! Leaving my kiddos is a source of stress for me because they provide me with so much strength.

God has plans for his future that dwarfs his past... thanks be to God that Jesus came to give us life, and that abundantly. (John 10:10). Praying the Spirit awakens and empowers Scotts spirit to take hold of life and hope. (Thank you, my friend, Gwen Peters for these perfect words at the perfect time this morning)

There are two parallel universes in this story. There is me at the hospital caring for my husband, and there is me that is a mom and trying to maintain some sanity and safety at home. I opened both universes to everyone I knew, and everyone they know.

December 29

Thanks for riding this roller coaster with me. Monday was a very dark day for me. Maybe the darkest ever. I couldn't seem to pull out of a negative thought nose dive. So when friends and family checked in and asked how I was doing, I was honest with them. My brother called me immediately and then he and my sister-in-law endured a sobbing, stuffed nose unintelligible conversation with me at the hardest moments that evening. This is very out of character for me to emote so much, but man! A rush of bad news followed by more bad news, and then further bad news, on zero sleep. As usual, Jay and Meri said exactly the right things and got me through it. Thank you to everyone who has answered my moment of weakness phone calls. I'm thankful you let me lay it all on you for a while.

Fast forward to the next morning, and a fresh perspective as well as some glimmers of hope. Scott recovered remarkably quick from his brain bleed. Some effects remain, like short-term memory loss, but in time will heal.

His charm has not been affected. I called in at 3 am to check on him, and she expressed how sweet he is.

We are back on the road to getting him home. Strength is the primary obstacle. He's been here more than 2 weeks now, and part of it in i.c.u. or intubated, or in cardiac arrest...that's a lot for one dude.

I have spoken with multiple doctors and a specialist this morning who are confident that they can give him the care that he needs. Our doctor today and yesterday ordered a massive amount of labs to rule things out and try to get to the bottom of why the heparin didn't work. The hematologist doesn't advise any blood thinners at all until he is certain the brain bleed is stable. Another ct scan tomorrow morning to compare. I welcomed this news because others have mentioned getting him started again on a low dose, but it just feels too risky.

My little lane to my house has become a highway with traffic coming and going. Even my dog is being looked after. Sometimes the kids say, "We don't know who that was but they brought x-y-z..." I also finally got brave enough to look at our go fund me account. I wasn't sure how I'd react knowing that people who budget for every dollar they earn instead chose to give some to my family. As I expected, it hurt my heart and warmed my heart at the same time.

I make no guarantees that we won't hit another hill on this coaster. I can only promise, I will try not to throw up on you.

Once again, he was on the (potential) road to recovery. Once again, we were eager to graduate out of the ICU. Once again, we were trying to gain strength and abilities with the hope of going home (eventually). There was a light at the end of a very long tunnel, and the light wasn't yet visible.

I was making plans to stay in Portland. I would stay with our cousin Liz, and her wife Joelle while Scott was taken care of at OHSU. I drove home to pack a bag full of everything I would need. I wasn't looking forward to being so far away from the kids, and unable to drive back and forth from the hospital to see them, but I tried to remind myself that this is the role I needed to fill.

Chapter 17

While I wasn't thrilled with all of the doctors at Samaritan, the nurses were, for the most part, exceptional. They took it upon themselves to help him get the procedure he needed.

From what I understand, some of his weight gain was fluid. His nurses determined that by administering Lasix, they could eliminate a lot of that fluid in a short amount of time and get his weight down enough so that the IVC filter could be done in Corvallis.

It worked.

Doctors let us know that he had hit the mark and could have the procedure. It was scheduled and we were not going to have to transfer to Portland.

I updated my previous post. Many never saw it.

we are living moment to moment and things are a-changing on the fly. He is now able to have the ivc filter procedure in Corvallis. As of now we are staying here. (End of update)

As we neared the day and time of the procedure, we learned that there had been yet another hiccup. One hospital hand hadn't talked to the other, and so his procedure never actually got on the schedule. Again, I wondered, is this normal? Does everyone go through this chaos when someone's life is at risk? Does it ever go smoothly and everything fall into place? I explained the circumstances to everyone following the story.

December 28th, 2021

Scott just said, "Tell everyone to say a prayer for me."   I smirked and said, Babe, people have been praying nonstop for weeks. But he doesn't know what I know...not yet.

First batch of good news, CT scan shows that the brain bleeds are unchanged. He seems to have recovered quite well from the bleeding. He is improving on his neurological tests every time. We both got a good night sleep too. He's anxious to get the show on the road this morning.

There were some miscommunications in the ICU among doctors here and interventional radiology where the procedure will be done. An order was never put in, the capability is there, then it isn't, then it is again, etc. There is no set time but it is finally a go (until it isn't again!! but if that happens it won't be pretty) I'm told that the setup takes longer than the procedure which is relatively simple. Simple?

There are still many steps to take for him to be able to come home. The brain bleeds have put a stop to any anticoagulation of his blood, which is necessary to control his clotting issue. Guess how many time I've heard the phrase, "We're between a rock and a hard place" and from how many different doctors   The filter will protect him from his leg clots traveling to his lungs, however he still has clots already in his lungs, so they have to deal with those before they become pulmonary embolisms. The neurologist has okayed a return to anticoagulation, however, I'm not so sure. I'm no doctor, but so far anytime they've told me there's a risk of something bad, the something bad has materialized. Sooooo......

Once the filter procedure is done, he will be PCU status, not ICU status. Progress! Physical therapy will return to get him back functioning physically, and the process begins again. I keep telling him to picture himself walking through our front door. He says he is.

I had coffee with a patient this morning who was told he had a month to live and he's two weeks in. he's 43, with a son in Roseburg who has a baby on the way. I told him to just keep living, and make sure to send a card to the hospital every week that says, "Still here."

Also spoke with a woman coming in for a procedure to figure out why she's so severely short of breath. She has A-fib, so we bonded.

I'm trying to spread the love that's been showered upon me, just in case they don't have what I have. You.

The nurses saved the day once again and put a rush on getting him on the schedule. He was wheeled away, and soon wheeled back into the ICU with a filter inside of him. I breathed relief knowing he was covered while not on blood thinners. It seems that every time relief comes, the "why are we even here" anger returns too. I took to my journal, which by now was no longer hand written:

So am I supposed to just sit here? Sit here and wait...wait for you to be ready to go home? Wait for you to have another massive life-threatening event? The waiting is the worst. Being patient is challenging.

You've been sleeping since I got here this morning. You took about a 2-hour nap after I arrived, woke up, wet your bed, and went back to sleep. I left to go get some errands done. I picked up a birthday present for Staci, still intending to pop into her birthday party. I dropped off our recycling, and went to work for about an hour. I finally shared your medical struggles with our listeners. On-air and via social media, leaving out the dignity-sucking parts that I know you wouldn't want people to know...like wetting your bed. Our go fund me instantly jumped by $3000. Over the years you've been so giving of your time, your resources, and your humor, I think people want to make sure you know how loved you are. I love hearing the stories of their impression of you. "He always had a smile on his face when I saw him in town." "See what happens when you blame Angie for everything! Get well soon." "Everyone at Little Ceasars is praying."

You are probably the most famous man in town. Everybody knows Scott Schuler. Not only did you grow up and graduate high school in Albany, but you also became the morning show host on your hometown radio station. Even the mayor isn't that famous.

You're confused today. Not sure where you are. Can't remember the year. Your most recent answer when asked what year it is was "'81 to '89."

The nurse thinks the confusion could be caused by co2 retention from not exhaling enough co2. This means, it's not a neurological issue, which is good news. I seek out the good news, even in tiny doses.

I talk like you'll go home. I talk about the Christmas presents you have to open. I did well this year. You're going to love them. I got you a new

Dewalt Drill set that came with a free blue tooth radio. I still have your birthday present to assemble in the laundry room. it's a patio umbrella with l.e.d. lights for over the hot tub.

You have missed almost all of December. Your birthday is on the 18th, Christmas, and tomorrow is New Year's Eve. You're still here, you're still sick, and I still have no idea when you can come home or if another life-threatening event awaits. I don't think I can take another one of those phone calls. The last one just about destroyed me.

The kids are doing great until they're not. Lincoln is a rock, and he makes sure to tell me. "I'm really doing quite well with this, Mommy." He still calls me Mommy at 15 years old.

I asked him the other night if he were allowed, would he want to visit you. He pondered the question for a minute, moving his mouth to one side of his face, and looking up at the ceiling.

"I feel like, I'm doing so well, and if I saw him, I don't think I could keep doing so well." he said after a minute. I told him that made a lot of sense, and I understood.

They can't do anything wrong. Whatever misbehavior may arise, I have to consider that it might be a reaction to all the weirdness surrounding them. Their world has been rattled, tossed in the air, and spiked like a football these past few weeks. Daddy isn't there, and now Mommy isn't there. We run as a pack. We are always together. Being separated has been hard on us all.

Before you coded, I fulfilled a wish I'd had for several years. Our children love their cuddles. There is always at least one child sleeping with us. I had built a platform for Loxley's toddler bed that lifted it to the same height as our bed. I placed it right next to my side of the bed. So that it became an extension of our bed. She has outgrown it though. Sunny had an extra double bed underneath her loft bed in her room. She wanted more space. I grabbed a tape measure. With a shift of just 4 inches, I could fit that double bed next to our bed, creating a massive family bed. Normally I would have run this by you. You would have probably protested, and I would have done it anyway, but with you away in the hospital, I did it anyway. Most nights now, there are at least 3 children, sometimes 4, one night 5 sleeping in our room, and it's glorious. I know they feel safe in there, and with so much uncertainty, I try to provide security where I can.

The nights are the hardest, as they always are. The emotions come out at night. Sunny misses you and she fears going back to our homeschool co-op knowing that people will ask her about you. It reminds me of when I used to get mad when people would ask "How are you feeling" whenever I was pregnant. I told Sunny what you told me. That they only ask because they care, so let them care about you. I don't know why that was so hard for me to do. I suppose I can blame hormones.

Anthem seems fine. He spends his days pestering his siblings and riding his hoverboard. I know he misses me and is worried about you. He buries himself in things he loves like drawing, pestering, and hoverboarding.

Braddock has little breakdowns over a typical 6-year-old's worries. He's been a regular in my new family bed. He asks me each night to "throw me on the bed...but spin me first." We do that a few times. He has always wanted to lay or sleep with me, now he can whenever he likes.

Loxley is so sharp and aware. She's 4, so people have remarked that she probably doesn't even know what's going on. She does though. She's incredibly observant, often bringing up things she's noticed that I didn't think possibly could.

"I don't want you to go to the hospital." she said last night. As I said, nights are the hardest.

"Why did you go to jail, Mommy?" She also said. Maybe she's confusing a jail and hospital. This one is starting to feel very similar. Not that I've ever been to jail, but I imagine it would feel something like this. I can come and go, but you can't.

Tomorrow you will have been in the hospital for 3 weeks. In a bed, hooked up to everything, which means you haven't been outside for 3 weeks. You died, got brought back, suffered a stroke, and haven't been able to breathe. Sounds like jail to me.

I'm here to try and keep your spirits up. Some days I just sit here and write, and try to calm your anxieties.

When I first came in to see you after receiving that 6 am call that I should "come now," I held your hand. While you were on life support for an entire day, I held your hand. After they removed the tube in your throat, I held your hand. To help you sleep, I held your hand.

Before you were transferred to Corvallis and were still in wait at the Lebanon E.R., you asked me to hold your hand. You were in a very uncomfortable bed in the room, and I was about to head home. At this point in the story, I was mostly just annoyed. Annoyed with you for not making time for your health, because now, we were forced to make time for your illness. You held out your hand as though asking me to hold it.

"Why?" I said in an annoyed tone.

"Because, it feels good." you responded.

I think back to this moment because you were about to take an ambulance transport to be admitted for blood clots. I was annoyed, and I think maybe you were scared. Of course, you wouldn't say the words, "I'm scared." Big strong man and all. But I think maybe you weren't letting on how serious this was. Maybe the doctor said, or maybe you just knew that we were in for a major turn.

Chapter 18

The days in the hospital were long for Scott. He wasn't sleeping well at night still. I would call to check on him in the night and the nurses, sometimes sounding fed up would tell me that he was wide awake and wanting turned. His butt still hurt. Sitting, but mostly lying in bed all day will do that. His physical therapists were getting him in his chair, but his progress was slow and although sick of the hospital, he didn't seem in any hurry to get to a point physically of coming home. He still didn't get up to use the bathroom and relied on nurses (or me and once or twice one of his visitors) to get to him in time with the urinal. The first time it was me, I joked "You know, there's no going back from this. I'm no longer your wife, I'm your nurse maid from here on out."

I was racking my brain for something each day for him to look forward to, to ease the dullness of his days staring at cream/off white walls and an elevated television.

I reached out to my friend Amy Krahn. She and her husband own Royal Riverside Farm, a Dairy farm in Albany. We get their delicious milk for our family each week. Scott had mentioned that he would like some of their milk. In addition to glass bottled milk, they also do individual servings called "chugs." Their chocolate is delicious and they seasonally offer other flavors. I asked if they would be willing to provide some milk for me to take to Scott each day on my visit. We still had no idea how much longer he would be admitted.

12/31/21 9:54 am

Amy Krahn

We are praying for you guys and especially for Scott. I wait patiently for your updates on social media, thank you for keeping us updated. In terms of providing milk for Scott in the hospital...we were thinking individual chugs or maybe quarts would be better? That way you can just throw away the plastic when you're done and don't have to worry about the glass bottles. Plus it is much easier to store in a small refrigerator that way. Can we deliver them right to the hospital? Do you want to stop by the farm to get them? Tell me what works best for you and we will make it happen.

Me: *I will stop by. I've got a million bottles to return. Are you open today or should I come next week?*

Amy: *I am open today. I can get all of the milk for Scott to you at that time and also any milk you want for the family.*

I love to help people. It is my greatest joy. I've learned that I am not the only one that feels that way. I often tell people that they have blessed me by allowing me to be of service. I truly felt that I was now blessing so many by allowing them to be of service to me.

When I arrived at the farm, I was wrapped in one of Amy's fabulous hugs. I gave her an in person update, and loaded up a couple of flats of milk, both white and chocolate. Likely, it had been in the cow just hours earlier, that's how fresh this milk is.

Each day, I took Scott 2 chugs. It started out as white and chocolate, but he asked for just chocolate within a day or two. His nurses would place his "evening chug" in their nursing station refrigerator and make sure he got it as dessert each night after I left.

I had settled into a routine again.

Back at work, I was covering the morning show, grateful to to give Glenn Nobel a somewhat normal day instead of 2 weeks of marathon broadcasting. Our paths didn't cross a lot at the station. When they did, I gave him updates. He also asked to visit Scott.

When someone asks to visit, I would give my husband the final say. There were certain people he was okay with them seeing him in his current state. His pride would not allow others to see him in such a state. Once approved, I would give the visitor fair warning about what to expect. You might see his balls, and you'll definitely see his naked butt. You may be asked to grab the urinal at a moment's notice if he can't hit the call button in time. He's not much for conversation right now, so you'll be doing most of the talking, but probably you'll just watch TV with him.

His friends didn't mind any of this. Or if they did, they didn't say.

His friend, Steve "Kazoo" Haley was the first besides me, his sister, and Alex Remily to pay Scott a visit. After that is was some of his oldest and truest friends that marched in. As people were asking me if they could visit Scott, I asked my husband if there was anyone in particular he wanted to see.

"Bingham." Was his answer.

I think I knew he would say him. Scott Bingham is easy going, mellow, non-judgmental, and I think my husband knew that Scott would not lecture him (as I had been doing so much). Scott would be happy to sit in a room, and make small talk.

I sent a text to Scott Bingham, who is "Bing Daddy" in my phone.

"Scott doesn't want to see anyone really, except you and Kazoo. Are you available?

Scott Bingham: *"you bet! I would love to! What do I need to do?"*

I told him to pick a day that worked for him. My husband's schedule was pretty open.

Because of Covid, the two of us couldn't be in the room at the same time, so I headed to work in anticipation of Bingham's visit. This became my new routine. I started a schedule of visitors each day and when they were sitting with my husband, I would head into work the next town over.

It was not difficult to schedule, as only one visitor was allowed each day, and I had requests from several people wanting to see him. Scott's sister, and his Dad would fill in any gaps, so there wasn't a day that he didn't have someone's company besides mine.

In addition to visiting my husband, Scott Bingham and Kazoo took care of some work at my house. They winterized our above ground swimming pool, and also took care of some of the mess left by the concrete layers who had poured the slab for our shop just before Scott got sick.

My father in law, John Schuler and his wife Leslie unexpectedly came out to the house. I happened to be there when they arrived. They asked if there was anything that needed done. They took care of buttoning up Christmas lights and general property maintenance that day. John also fixed my garage door which hadn't been closing properly. I've always been able to rely on my father in law. He's bailed me out on numerous occasions. No less than twice when my car broke down or was breaking down, he came to my rescue. I always think of him when I'm fueling up. The last time my car was having issues, he looked at my ¼ tank full gas gauge and scolded me for having it so "empty."

After exiting for a visitor, I headed to work one afternoon. Sometimes when I'm downloading audio, I'll scoll facebook. A marketplace listing for a twin over full bunk bed popped up. I clicked on it. It was in great condition, taken apart, and the price was right. I had been looking for exactly this for Lincoln, who often has friends sleep over. Life was going on. The timing though, plus, I wasn't sure I could fit it in my Excursion. I called John, my father in law.

"What are you doing today?" I asked.

"Not much. What are you doing?"

I asked if he would like to come pick me up, drive me to Corvallis, and help me load and deliver a bunk bed to my house. Without hesitation, he agreed. He pulled into the radio station parking lot within about 30 minutes. We enjoyed the drive, chatting the whole way.

The man that had listed the bunk bed lived in a clean, modest house. He was also kind, and very generous. He gave me a slight discount and had also only taken the bed apart to a manageable degree, understanding someone would have to reassemble it, making it relatively easy. He bagged up all the small parts, and he and his son helped us load it. We had a mutual friend too. Jack Burright. I explained that Jack had been a reliable shoulder for me the past few weeks.

Jack is my kids' karate instructor. A former law enforcement officer, he commands respect and hard work from those in his classes. Loxley thinks he looks like Pat Sajak from Wheel of Fortune.

Nearly every day I had a message from Jack asking about my condition. He was worried about my physical and mental health. Scott had a visitor one day following his stroke. I was caught up at work and needed a different focus. My sister in law, having been at my house so much hadn't even put up her own Christmas tree yet. I called my niece, she told me how to get into the house, and I got to work trying to Christmas up her place. While I was there, Jack called me. We talked almost the entire time I cleaned. Maybe for an hour or more. I spilled my guts about everything. My ability to avoid the painful admissions no longer existed. I'm still not sure why he was the one I confessed everything to. I suppose he called at exactly the right time that I needed to. It was interesting to me how so many people in my life that filled a certain role took on an entirely new role throughout Scott's hospitalization. This man, that had been our instructor for years, had seen an opening to become more. His messages of support wouldn't stop for many more months.

I was rolling into the hospital each day, armed with farm fresh milk chugs at around 8 am. Having put the house back together, loved on whichever kiddos were awake, our pace and schedule now a routine.

Scott was usually sitting up in his chair, eager to show me, "look, I'm out of bed." But ready to be back in it as soon as I arrived.

Sometimes, I would arrive in time for his physical therapy, but I would often miss the doctors who made their rounds earlier than I arrived. I adjusted my schedule to try to catch them. When Scott relayed the information to me from the doctors, I knew that he was either holding some of it back, not relaying it properly, or making some of it up. He still suffered memory loss and confusion from the stroke at this point, so I knew that I needed to talk with the doctors directly.

In the immediate days after his stroke, he was really enjoyable to be around. My husband is not a great communicator in everyday life, but after his stroke, forgive me, he wouldn't shut up, and I loved it.

Every thought he had he gave words to. Some of it was nonsense, but it was all jolly and fun. I would come home at night and tell the kids stories about how Daddy thought he was at the airport today, or the Sheriff's office, or the library, but not at the hospital. A little bit of light heartedness on top of the fear. Within a week or so, though, he began to fall into somewhat of a depression. He stopped communicating with me, unless I pried, but even when I did pull answers from him they were rarely more than 1 word or 2. Mostly he would respond with "I don't know," or "I don't want to talk about it." When I told stories of my day, he wouldn't hardly acknowledge that I'd even spoken. I think that's why I started writing this book. There was no one to talk to on my visits to his room.

We did work on his memory. He was having trouble remembering some of our kids' names. He didn't remember giving stockings full of goodies on Christmas Eve to the hospital staff, and he was confusing other people too.

He announced one day that Matt Medina had come to visit him.

We haven't seen or spoken to Matt Medina in years. He is a friend who used to live locally and there was a season in our life when we saw him regularly but it had probably been 10 or more years since then.

"Matt Medina didn't visit you," I said.

"Really!?"

"Not Matt Medina, Matt...um...Matt McCormick I meant."

I had heard the name Matt McCormick a time or two. This was a person that had gone to high school with my husband. I may have met him once in our 20 plus years together.

"Nope." I said.

He eventually remembered his friend Alex's visit, and even Kazoo.

My theory (as I told Scott Bingham in a text) was that he was able to see the "tt" in a name and Scott Bingham's face, but couldn't come up with "Scott" so he said that it was "Matt."

It was kind of fun and interesting to analyze the misfires in his brain. I did wonder if this was all permanent, but the doctors (who I was now catching as long as I arrived by 7 am) would reassure me that the human brain is amazing and would rewire itself. It would just take time.

Chapter 19

At the radio station, everyone was eager for updates each day when I arrived. It was generally around lunch time as that was when his visitors arrived. Some would leave their jobs, or sacrifice their sleep to sit with my husband, and I was profoundly grateful to them.

Usually my co-workers would pop their heads into the studio and ask about Scott. I gave full updates to each person, never troubled to repeat the same story. The fact that they cared so much was not a burden. I would also give routine updates during the morning show, including, once a day paraphrasing the entire ordeal for new listeners, or those who hadn't heard.

Radio listeners come in different forms. Some listen religiously, others punch the dial, and still others tune in sporadically. I took all of them into consideration in my transparent commentary about my husband's health crisis. A significant number of medical professionals listen to our radio station, so I was delighted to be able to tell positive stories about our Samaritan hospital experience. I named the nurses and doctors specifically knowing their friends and family may also be listening. I truly love small town radio.

Cards were pouring in for Scott. Each day after work, I would return to visit him for dinner (another part of my routine) and deliver his cards. His reaction wasn't over the top. Some he simply read and set aside. Some brought him to tears. Some I read to him. I saved each and every card he received in a journal. I also shared them on the air and thanked the individuals, families and businesses that had taken the time to write to him and encourage him.

Elizabeth works in our front office. She was fielding calls and cards for Scott. She would hand over the stack of well wishes each day when I arrived.

"He's the reason I have everything I have." She tearfully confessed to me about Scott one morning."

She explained that she had broken down on more than one occasion throughout the past few weeks of Scott's illness out of worry for him.

When Elizabeth had come to work at the radio station, she was a single mother living in a drafty trailer in a seedy part of town.

Scott encouraged her to apply for a Habitat for Humanity home. He was a board member and felt that her situation was exactly right to receive a home. She was involved in the build which turned out to be a remodeled Habitat Home. We were there the day she received the keys.

He also pointed her in the direction of a safe vehicle to purchase for her and her daughter Amelia. Friends of ours had been selling an SUV and Elizabeth was able to purchase it outright with Scott's help.

Wendy on our sales staff had witnessed my relationship with Scott in its early stages, and had attended our wedding 18 years prior.

Jason had been in our building for more than a decade, advancing from sales to a management roll overseeing two markets. He spoke with me daily, and I vented and cried to him on several visits. He was understanding, and accommodating to my schedule. I was conscious to continue performing well despite the challenges. Whether they cared, or not, I continued to keep our listeners apprised of Scott's health.

Chapter 20

Another holiday, New Year's Eve arrived. Having spent breakfast and dinner with my husband, headed to work in between, I was able to celebrate with my kids at home.

My daughter's friend, Chloe was spending the night. Her mom was also in the hospital. Brandy and Kyle had been so generous throughout the holidays, even supporting us with a financial gift, but all the while, Brandy was suffering physically. She didn't tell me because she felt like I had enough to worry about, but she was being admitted for complications from an autoimmune disease (that I wasn't even aware she had).

We celebrated the end of 2021 with a late night dance party. I kept any trouble about Scott to myself and just enjoyed a night of silliness with my kids. We also sent videos to Chloe's mom in the hospital. She has 2 other children, and I offered to go get them if needed. Her fiancé, Kyle was taking good care of the boys.

As I observed the hospital activity, I began to wonder...why there was only a bed and a chair in my husband's room. The worst thing for him, from what I understand, is immobility. He needs to stand up, to walk around. The room was the size of an average living room with too much furniture. He was required to mask while walking in the hall, and drag his i.v. drip with him. At nearly 500 pounds, it was an obvious struggle. Yet here he sat, or lay all day long with only a few laps around the nurses station when physical therapy time rolled around once a day.

This frustrated me. I began to wonder if a hospital is just a place to go and die, and not to go and become well. My husband needs activity and movement, not laying around watching television. That is what landed him here in the first place.

The Christmas decorations had long been put away and it was now 2022. Scott remained in the hospital, in his room, and I dutifully visited him each day for breakfast and dinner with a break for work in the middle and my evenings with the kids. The blessing that all of this had happened over our holiday break was not lost on me. There was no responsibility of school work, no homeschool co-op, and no sports to attend. As challenging as coordinating my days between hospital, work, home, and other duties was, it could have been much more difficult if the timing had been different.

We were now coming upon a return to our "Monday school," our homeschool co-op. All 5 kids attend, and I teach 2 classes. Most of my kids are in my classes as well as children of other families that home school. It's really lovely to have a community of like-minded parents and grandparents that grow to love my children, and I grow to love theirs.

There had been a Christmas party for the co-op. I was not able to take my kids. I reached out to my Mother in law and Sister in law. I knew they would enjoy the day with the kids, and get to meet these families that held us up in such genuine, loving prayer.

Sunny, 11 at the time, was concerned that she would be asked "How are you?" and that it would cause her to break down. I let Katie Forrest know. Katie is the lead board member of the co-op and explained that everyone would just be delighted to see the kids. I knew that they would get lost in the festivities and probably have a wonderful time. They did. Sunny won a miniature waffle iron in the white elephant gift exchange and came home with the broadest smile.

It would have been easy to blow off the party, rather than make arrangements for them to go, but I really made the effort throughout the month of my husband's hospitalization to keep my kids' lives as normal as possible. So much had been turned upside down for them, I wanted them to have pleasant memories of the season we were in.

The co-op winter formal dance had also taken place in that time. I remember sitting in my husband's hospital room, shopping online for formal wear that Lincoln, 15 at the time would agree to wear. We had gotten him a phone for his 15th birthday, so I sent him texts with outfits I thought he would like. He picked a checkered, mustard colored vest over a white shirt, and black jeans. That's as formal as he would get.

I explained to Scott on the day of the dance that I wouldn't be back for my dinner visit. That Lincoln had a dance. After racing into work, I headed home to clean my car, which would serve as the limousine.

Lincoln, his best friends, Dylan and Gabe, and his cousin Samantha got ready for the dance at our house. I shot video of everything. In my opinion, the dance itself is only part of the fun. The getting ready, the pictures, the drive there, and the drive home are also important to make memorable.

Because our co-op is small compared to a school, the moms cook dinner for the teens and start the evening with a formal sit down dinner. I blew that one. I mistook the time, and we arrived after dinner. The kids didn't seem too bummed. I had purchased beverages and snacks for the drive so they had something in their tummies.

I stayed and chaperoned, and was able to speak with some of the moms that I hardly knew. You see, on co-op days, we moms bounce from class to class, teaching or helping, and then cleaning up the church, and hardly have time to make conversation except for passing smiles and pleasantries.

I talked that night at length with Gretta. Gretta is skilled in conversation and those are my favorite people to talk to. She asked me questions, responded to my answers, and offered her own insight from her experiences. Gretta had always intimidated me just a bit. She seemed somehow more evolved than me, and that always causes me to retreat. I am a work in progress, and know that this is something I need to work on. I found out that night that Greta has spent her adulthood healing, much like me. We had numerous family dynamics in common and she gave me hope with no judgment that night. I could spend an entire week talking with Greta and still not have had enough.

I also spoke with my sweet friend, Jenny. Jenny had helped in my "Geography Through Art" class the previous year, and I enjoyed her company and assistance so much that we became fast friends. Just seeing her brought me comfort. And Kathleen. Her youngest and my youngest are pals, and Kathleen has such a divine, comforting nature, I almost don't know how to behave around her. Her children all have it too, and I often wonder how one achieves that. Maybe it's not something to achieve but simply something to be.

My walls had been knocked down, and I was so relieved and felt so light as a result. Openly discussing all the things that I had been hiding was the healing that I needed. Who knew?!

January 6th

Christmas break ended and brought a return to work for me, and school and work for me and the kids. We started our homeschool co-op again this week. We didn't have to but wanted to, and I'm patting myself on the back for that decision because it was something we all needed. I was able to thank all of the families there who have been like a warm blanket to us. I think I bumbled my way through it, but I hope that's what came across.

Scott is still in Corvallis hospital. He was never transferred to OHSU. I get that question a lot and I'm sorry for the confusion. That day that they intended to transfer him was really really scattered. Corvallis was able to do the necessary procedure there so there was no need for the transfer. From what I've heard, we're fortunate to even have a hospital bed right now, and hopefully, we can free one up shortly.

I hesitate to give any timelines because the doctors hesitate to give me any timelines. When they do, they often change, or a different doctor says something different, and then I have to untell. I did speak to his Dr (He has several though) yesterday morning. They are monitoring him as they have restarted him on heparin (as of Monday night, I believe) and coumadin (whoa that's the first time I spelled that right). The heparin immediately thins his blood, the coumadin will become therapeutic in a few days, so they bridge the two. They are monitoring him in the event of another bleed, as well as clotting. (I tell him every night, No bleeding, no clotting and get good rest) They are not ready to move him to a care facility where if something traumatic occurs, they may not be equipped to act quickly enough. We were fortunate that he was in ICU already and that Julie was right there, and aware the minute his brain started bleeding. They were able to keep the damage minimal.

I don't tell you everything. I can't. So much would be guesswork. Questions I can't answer, and neither can anyone else (I've asked). "How long" questions mostly. A lot of it depends on him, his body, the medication, and whatever else the universe has in store for him. He is improving every day physically. He is not short of breath like he was the week after he coded, and before his stroke, so the lung clots are not causing the problems they were. The leg clots are stable and the filter in his valve will keep them away from his lungs. The treatment is the treatment and I believe he is in very good hands. I try to cross paths each day with the Doctor, the physical therapist, and the occupational therapist. After I visit, I head to work. After work, I usually head home to visit the kids and keep them on track with school. Then I head back to the hospital to visit for the afternoon. (except for yesterday, I threw in a couple crowns and fillings to shake things up a little bit) I usually stay until dinner, and then head home to put the house back together. So the meal train is saving my life. Although Lincoln and Sunny are very capable of making meals (they both love to cook, and Lincoln has several Hello Fresh recipes waiting in the fridge.) I don't want them to have to do that every night. I promise though, they wouldn't mind.

So the days are pretty full, but that's nothing new for us, We like to use all the hours Sunny, Anthem, and Braddock's ' Distance Learning program has been very kind, cutting us some slack and even providing a gas card to help us out. We've been with Paisley since Lincoln was in 2nd grade, and their teacher is like family. I'm so thankful for them.

Life didn't stop and other things have come up. Things that Scott would normally handle, or that I would discuss with him but I've had to step up. I don't want to worry him with anything right now. I take the challenges as an opportunity to grow, and definitely see them as a blessing.

If you have seen me and ask how I am, I will tell you how I am at that moment. I usually have myself together. There are moments where I wallow a little bit in my worries and fears. I don't feel bad and just must need to do that in between being everything to everyone. I can take a hit, and recover, so I'm happy to be the first line of defense.

When I get home, the kids always ask how Daddy is. You may not know this, but even Lincoln, at 15, still calls us Daddy and Mommy. I give them updates, and they hear me on the phone with people too. I do stay strong around them because I want them to feel that it's okay for them to be emotional. If I'm a wreck, they'll not want to make me sad, and they'll want to take care of me. Believe it or not, this helps me keep everything in perspective.

I've never doubted that Scott will heal, and come home to us, but at the same time, I have to prepare myself. It's a train wreck in my head sometimes. So I have to stop myself from imagining too far into the future. My favorite bible verse is -Don't worry about anything; instead, pray about everything. I still worry. That's hard to shut off, but I still pray.

If I don't answer a text, call, or message immediately, I'm pressed for time. I usually sit down later, and go back over everything and try to catch up though. I know that you care about Scott and me. I love how different people care. Some text/call every day because they care, and some don't text at all, they suspect I'm overwhelmed and don't want to add anything more. I appreciate the entire spectrum of how you choose to show you care. You're not doing it wrong no matter how you choose, so thank you.

Chapter 21

Two weeks had passed since Scott's December 26th stroke and after the doctors checked his scans, the put him back on blood thinners. He was put on the heparin drip, the same anticoagulant that didn't seem to make any difference nearly a month before, when this all started.

The goal was to transition to Coumadin. Weird! I had heard that word years earlier as a teenager. My Grandpa, "Poppy" had heart disease. He died when I was 15. He was on Coumadin the entirety of the time that I knew him. How is it now, my husband is on Coumadin? I will admit, I felt self-pity at this thought. He is 49 years old. He's not a Grandpa, "Poppy." Sure we had kids later in life. Our oldest was born when I was 30, and our youngest when I was 40.

I gathered myself though, and stayed the course.

The days seemed endless for Scott. Mentally, he was just barely surviving. The four walls of the hospital room were closing in. The milk chugs weren't enough to deter his depression. We needed to get him out of this place, and soon.

As a "non-jabbed" individual, his options for a transitional rehabilitation facility were limited. Everything was full and he would need a separate area away from other residents. My connection with a woman named Sheila at the facility locally didn't end up working out, but her effort deserved mention in this book.

One of my closest friends, Jill has a close friend of her own named Sheilah. Sheilah and I have crossed paths a dozen or so times over the years, exchanging a smile and a hello, but rarely anything more than that. I never knew very much about Sheilah other than she likes country music, because our interactions were usually at a concert.

In August of 2021, Jill invited me to a concert in Bend, about 90 or so miles from my house. I was going to hitch a ride with Sheilah, but when I decided to bring my daughters along, Sheilah wound up hitching a ride with me.

We made the 90-mile drive to Bend, making small talk, and getting to know each other. I mostly asked questions of her but offered my own story when prompted. The drive there was mostly uneventful. Upon arrival at the concert venue, where neither of us had ever been, we did have to stop and ask where we were supposed to park. We drove around lost for a little while.

We met up with Jill, and the other girls that had made the trip for her birthday, and the group of us stayed at a rental house. I slept in a bunk bed with my 4-year-old, so sleeping is a bit of an overstatement.

After an awesome Old Dominion concert and a relatively sleepless night, we started our drive home. My 4-year-old is known for getting car sick on long car rides, so we were careful to take the curvy highway roads at a slow pace. Again we made small talk and continued getting to know each other. I had already determined that Sheilah and I could be friends if she'd have me.

Upon returning to the Willamette Valley, nearing Foster Lake, the projectile vomit from the backseat happened. We had brought some supplies, but they were scattered. The wise Sheilah had a small package of wipes in her purse. I used every one. We switched my daughter into her brother's empty car seat and finished the remainder of the drive home, about 20 more minutes.

The next day at work, I received a text from Sheilah, whose number I didn't have so I didn't recognize it. She was asking how my daughter was doing after our eventful landing the day before. It touched my heart that she was following up even after my daughter barfed on her.

It just so happens that Sheila works at one of the local rehabilitation facilities. Had we not made that whirlwind trip, I wouldn't have had the connection I now have with her. She texted me the day Scott's heart stopped.

December 17

Sheilah: Thinking of you and your family...please let me know if you need anything. I'd be happy to help.

The day before Christmas, I received a card from her with a financial contribution. I texted her immediately

December 24

Me: Good morning, Sheilah. I just opened your card. That is beyond kind. I just want you to know I think you are lovely. I told Jill after our road trip, I regretted not having gotten to know you before. She of course agreed with everything I said. Thank you for your generosity and your friendship.

Sheilah: You are very welcome and I thought the same...glad to call you my friend.

I reached out again just after the New Year when it was time to consider Scott's transition to coming home.

January 1

Mr: Hi Sheilah, Scott will be moving to a care facility in the coming week. Should I shoot for Avermere? Are there going to beds available? I don't know anything about anything.

Sheilah: You have the hospital do a referral to us and admissions will go from there.

Of consideration when selecting a care facility was proximity to home, and visitation rules. Scott really wanted to see the kids, so we wanted to make sure that was an option.

Me: What is the visitation policy?

Sheilah: Visitors are allowed, just get temperature at the door. No limit on time, no limit on people. Kids okay too.

Me: You just made me so happy.

We requested a referral of Scott's hospital case worker who got right to work. He was very attentive and communicative and kept us up to speed with all of the developments, good or bad. I texted Sheilah with an update.

January 6

Me: Avermere no beds, and vaccination status is an issue. Private room at a facility in Dallas is all case worker could find.
Sheilah: I'm having Brenna our admit person call dc planner again
Sheilah: Looks like he's coming next week per admissions
Me: Well you are a girl that gets things done. Amazing news.
January 11
Me: No dice again. Avermere has cancelled us. Gov Brown's new restrictions to blame I'm told. Checking other places but I'm betting it's the same. Thank you, still for all your help.
Sheilah: You're welcome...I feel bad but we have an outbreak.

Our only option now was to take him home and have home health nurses pay daily visits. I knew that besides medicating him, his progress had completely stalled at the hospital and he needed to be home to heal.

His buddy, Charlie was coming regularly for visits. Charlie works nearby and had become a voice of encouragement for Scott. If there was a day when a visitor wasn't scheduled, Charlie would fill it. Nothing bothered Charlie about seeing his friend in such a state. If it did bother him, he brushed it aside for the sake of helping my husband improve his health. Charlie was often in the room for physical or occupational therapy, and assisted with the process.

One afternoon, Scott was on the schedule for a shower. It fell to Charlie, who was visiting at the time to assist with that too. Without hesitation, this man helped my husband clean himself. It was the first shower Scott had since his arrival at the hospital. It's fun to think back to these close friends, hanging out in high school, maybe on the basketball court. I imagined them being told that one day, one would help the other take a shower. It may have gotten a few chuckles at the time, yet, here they were.

In anticipation of Scott's return home, we made some modifications to the house. Scott's right side was still not back to full speed, his stamina was limited, and a number of his faculties were shaky at best.

Sarah Boren, and Ken Hall, our neighbors to the north and south, installed shower bars, toilet bars, and electricity for a bidet. I thoroughly enjoyed shopping for a bidet if you don't mind me saying. As much a gift for me as for my husband.

I'm not sure what got into me, but the night before Scott was scheduled to come home, I completely rearranged our bedroom. I had been allowed to work from home at times since 2008 and had a home radio studio. Very few elements of it worked anymore, so I decided it was time to scrap it. I took the entire thing apart, put all the parts and pieces into a tote. I tore apart the desk, which was scrap lumber on top of an Ikea cube and a filing cabinet. The next morning, I took the computer portion to work, and dumped it in my office. This excessive amount of work was probably not something that I needed to do before Scott returned home, but when my environment feels uncertain, my therapy is to rearrange. It's always been my way. Besides, he needed room to get around with a walker which he would likely use for the foreseeable future.

Nearly 2 weeks after we rang in the new 2022 year, we were given the go ahead. His Coumadin was therapeutic, and I'm sure they needed the room. He was being booted out of Corvallis Good Samaritan hospital.

January 12th, I wrote this:

I made the drive from our house in Lebanon to Corvallis hospital blinded by tears. I made the drive in silent prayer. I made the drive uncertain of what was waiting for me at the end. I made the drive in the middle of the night. I made the drive in the early morning. I made the drive twice a day sometimes. I made the drive in snow, and rain. I made the drive with dear friends, to and from. I made the drive on Christmas eve and day, and New Years Eve and Day. I made the drive today in the sunshine, hopefully for the last time, and I drove home with my husband.

Aware, the entire time that this could be an entirely different day with entirely different activities because of an entirely different outcome. I savored each motion of getting this opportunity, that at times I wasn't certain we would have.

As wonderful as the staff at Good Sam has been, a hospital is no place to live, and he lived there for nearly a month. What he's been through physically may be nothing compared to what he's been through emotionally. I know our friends and family will want to hug him and love him, and we will welcome that sometime in the future, I have no doubt. For now, our little family needs some time to decompress. We have all put our tough faces on for a long time. Today, we are feeling all of it. Our kids will not be able to say anymore that they've never seen their Dad cry after today. Thank you for the gift of time together, just us.

As I'm sure you know, there's much more to the story.

Chapter 22

He was wheeled downstairs in a wheelchair while I brought our 2006 Ford Excursion to the main entrance. Such a weird feeling to not be living here at the hospital anymore. I wouldn't be back, at least, not voluntarily.

I scrolled my phone as I sat at the half circle, temporary parking area for picking up and dropping off. A young man appeared in the automatic doors with my husband in an oversized wheelchair. He brought him as close to the vehicle as he could and assisted him to a stand.

It took an eternity for Scott to climb into the vehicle. Even with the elevation of the curb, and what little strength he had, it was a struggle. He grasped the "Oh Shit" handle inside the door, and the young man assisted as much as he could. I grasped his free hand and tried to pull him inside, to no avail. ¼ inch at a time he was able to slide into the seat. I thought to myself, "We need an easier to traverse vehicle."

The temporary "Pick up/drop off" parking is undercover. January 12th was a sunny day. As soon as we were out from underneath the roof, Scott tipped his head back and rolled down the window.

He hadn't seen the sun, or breathed fresh air in more than a month. He hadn't seen anything of interest besides the four walls of his room, and a TV screen in that time either. I was trying to imagine what he was experiencing. It had to be almost heavenly. I imagined that he was wrestling with his thoughts. "Did I die? Did I actually die, and this is heaven?"

He kept his window down, and I didn't complain as I usually would have that it was cold. Whatever he wanted today.

"Take me to the uh...the uh...the place."

I tried to respectfully lead him to the right words.

"The place with the uh, the red. It's got the...the uh...the thing...the big...the big thing."

I just kept driving. He seemed to know the way.

"Turn right here."

I turned right.

"Keep going. Keep going."

I kept going.

"Here! It's right here. Right there!"

Burger King. He wanted to go to Burger King but couldn't find the words.

The line was 10 cars deep. Noon on a Wednesday, of course it was.

I pulled into the back of the line.

Anything he wanted today.

I put the Excursion in park. He started to cry.

I have only seen my husband cry on a couple of occasions.

If this had been that movie that I had been watching of my life playing out on the screen like it felt the entire time, there would have been some epic music playing that signified that this was the end of the movie. But he and I both knew this wasn't the end...it was just a new chapter.

I realized that I had been holding my breath for almost a month. Every bit of anger I felt at him left me. I only felt sadness. I wanted to heal him, to make him well. I reached over and grabbed his hand. He sobbed as we waited to order food that wasn't hospital food. We would eat it in the car, not the hospital.

I saw hope for our future. I hoped for a new energy from him. I hoped that he would see the err in his ways. I hoped that he would seek healing for his traumas from long ago that lead him here. Sitting in that drive up fast food line, I had hope.

The line was too long. We left, and headed home so he could see his kids for the first time in a month and start living again.